and I shall
    have some
peace there

Also by Margaret Roach

A Way to Garden

and I shall have some peace there

trading in the fast lane for my own dirt road

margaret roach

GRAND CENTRAL
PUBLISHING

NEW YORK   BOSTON

Copyright information continued on page 261.

Grand Central Publishing
Hachette Book Group
237 Park Avenue
New York, NY 10017

www.HachetteBookGroup.com

Printed in the United States of America

First Edition: February 2011

10 9 8 7 6 5 4 3 2 1

Grand Central Publishing is a division of Hachette Book Group, Inc.
The Grand Central Publishing name and logo is a trademark of Hachette Book Group, Inc.

Library of Congress Cataloging-in-Publication Data

Roach, Margaret.
    And I shall have some peace there : trading in the fast lane for my own dirt road / Margaret Roach. — 1st ed.
        p. cm.
    Summary: "Follows the journey of a woman who leaves her big city corporate life to find solitude and authenticity in nature"—Provided by the publisher.
    ISBN 978-0-446-55609-5
    1. Roach, Margaret. 2. Copake Falls (N.Y.)—Biography. 3. Country life—New York (State)—Copake Falls. 4. Solitude—New York (State)—Copake Falls. 5. Authenticity (Philosophy)—Case studies. 6. Nature—Psychological aspects—Case studies. 7. Women gardeners—New York (State)—Biography. 8. Women executives—New York (State)—New York (State)—Biography. 9. Career changes—New York (State)—New York (State)—Case studies.. 10. New York (N.Y.)—Biography. I. Title.
    F129.C775R63 2011
    974.7'1044092—dc22
    [B]
                            2010012413

For amazing Grace, whose own tale is already
one of magic, too.

May this life serve to awaken.

*

Fairy tales can come true, it can happen to you
If you're young at heart.
For it's hard, you will find, to be narrow of mind
If you're young at heart.

You can go to extremes with impossible schemes.
You can laugh when your dreams fall apart at the seams.
And life gets more exciting with each passing day.
And love is either in your heart or on its way.

—CAROLYN LEIGH, "YOUNG AT HEART"

*

I want to know my own will and to move on with it.
And I want, in the hushed moments,
When the nameless draws near,
To be among the wise ones—
or alone . . .

—RAINER MARIA RILKE, *RILKE'S BOOK OF HOURS: LOVE POEMS TO GOD;*
ANITA BARROWS AND JOANNA MACY TRANSLATION

and I shall
     have some
peace there

Chapter 1

Margaret Untethered
(A Preview)

We shall not cease from exploration
And the end of all our exploring
Will be to arrive where we started
And know the place for the first time.

—T. S. ELIOT, "LITTLE GIDDING,"
FOUR QUARTETS

SHE OF NOBODY ELSE'S BIDDING: That is who I am now—someone who has not done what anyone else said since July 2008, though not because I am either disobedient or a slacker. Hardly. Thirty-two years of corporate servitude are in my past, and there will be no more promotions or pay stubs, thrilling facts I celebrate with a long-overdue vigil for my self, a one-woman sit-in in the woods.

Friends and colleagues warned that I would become depressed, isolated, perhaps worse when I walked away from my lucrative, esteem-laden career as Executive Vice President, Editorial Director at Martha Stewart Living Omnimedia on the last day of 2007, leaving the peak earning years in my wake and relocating to my longtime weekend home and garden in a New York State hamlet where dairy cows not so long ago outnumbered people. Many stories of retreat are tales instigated by a trauma, or depression. I was never depressed in my old life; I was just strangely and terribly lonely, isolated despite being surrounded by six hundred colleagues daily, more than a quarter of whom worked for me, and living in a city of millions.

I was a big success, people told me, but the secret I never spoke in reply or anytime was my belief that I had long ago given up on me—the one whom others, in equations of family, love, and work, relied upon—choosing the easy route over a path toward things they don't necessarily pay you or pat you on the back for. I remember when it happened: In my insecure early twenties, already a college dropout and wanting the absolution of proving I was no dummy, I took a job that placed a bet on my intellect over creativity. It was the surer horse but (as with many favorites) a comparative dullard to that sexy long shot of allowing one's potential sufficient time to percolate. Could I write fiction, or be a photographer? We would never know; right then and there, I turned my back on possibility. Promotions at the newspaper I signed on to at first came easily, and suddenly I had fallen into the *burning ring of fire* (yes, *bound by wild desire*); money talked. True, the tether to the old life was mostly a financial one, its other shiny-but-searing edge the attachment to ego-fueling professional esteem. *And it burns, burns, burns.*

If I was so successful, I wanted to say back to my best friend and my accountant and the guy who cuts my hair and everyone else lovingly offering praise all those years, then why had I pushpinned a cryptic note to myself on the kitchen wall, a plaintive shorthand list called Tolerances, as in, how much can you tolerate of what for how long? Why were all my years-old diaries aching with phrases like *the hit-by-car feelings of my workday* and *Where is my creativity?* and that clincher, *Who or what am I waiting for?*

So from a role in *The Devil Wears Mara* (as in Max Mara; though I never asked one personal errand of an assistant in all my executive years, nor threw a coat or handbag at anybody), I finally walked away and shape-shifted to bumpkin-in-training in the mere flash of time it takes to drive 120 miles. Single, childless, and technically even pet free, I started up the road to start again in my garden in the woods.

Right away, though, I began hearing the voice that would keep asking for an answer I did not have: *Who am I if I am not mroach@marthastewart dot com any longer?* As if that were not enough, the confrontational facet of Margaret manifested as that raspy voice broadened its inquisition: If I am neither working nor in a personal partnership, in service to some master or another, *who am I?*

I am nothing more than a work in progress, thank you—the truest answer I have ever given to that question. I am just me, which is (apologies to my old friend Martha) a good thing, even without the stripes and status that my onetime titles and W-2s and all the other "accomplishments" seemed to imply. This latest incarnation, which is at once a simpler and a harder one, began just as the formative childhood version had—in stretchy, shapeless clothing, with most waking hours spent either on the floor puzzling things out or parked safely in the one same seat, trying to learn to focus the gaze, a bit of a bobblehead all over again.

Big fat lie:

As soon as I got out of my out-of-control city life, I got everything under control.

With my exit from the city and from corporate culture—from what had become my own place of disaffection despite astonishing views of the Empire State Building and the rest of the man-made majesty from up on high, twenty-four floors in the sky, where I sat—I had planned to go to heaven in a wheelbarrow of plants and creativity. Reality check: Forces bigger than myself have determined a different course these cataclysmic days. *To hell in a handbasket*, as Grandma liked to say, we were apparently meant to head instead. *Tra-la*.

Hard time on a cold floor during a rough recession might not sound seductive, but fair warning; the smell of homegrown home cooking and worse yet, of freedom, may prove to be contagious if small indignities that will surely surface can be overlooked, and then outlasted. The trick is learning to stay still.

Indeed, I awoke in my clothes the first wintry weeks more than just occasionally, and puttered other days away in my pajamas. (In those early months, the two categories of clothing looked different enough to be told apart.) I spent a considerable amount of time doing what I self-respectingly must assert was ruminating: repeatedly weighing a strengthening desire to pierce my navel at the tattoo place just five miles up the road, by the only traffic light within fifteen; mentally calculating the (prere-cession) run-rate of my inadequate savings while I categorized and then alphabetized an enormous CD collection on the living room floor; discarding twenty-nine of the thirty-seven pairs of jeans I'd accumulated somehow, even though I never wore jeans in my recent past life; matching up freezer containers with their lids and nesting them in size order the way a child learns from, and delights in, a set of colorful plastic stacking toys.

Craving solitude and invoking my right to self-determination, I had pulled my own rug out from under myself, and now I was sitting on it, wondering about the new math of 2008; about my new look; about *Who am I if I am not mroach@marthastewart dot com any longer?* The story went that I was now doing the things I'd never had the time to do, the things I'd shut down my life-line to income production and dropped out to make time for. Can these really be the things I never had time to do? *Are CDs and recycled yogurt and cottage cheese cups the guideposts on the true path?* Every journey must have its guides, its messengers—but these? *This is what you send me?*

WHAT DIGITAL RABBIT HOLE HAD LED ME to Andre Jordan, an eccentric British cartoonist, I do not know. But when I got there in late 2007, across a web of ISPs and DNSs and URLs, I found Andre had doodled five bold white tree trunks against a black background in one of many oddball illustrations on his blog that's aptly named A Beautiful Revolution. Beneath the trees, a hand-lettered inscription: *I've decided to go live in the woods (it's for the best).*

From this total stranger (now a dear friend and weekly

contributor to my garden blog, but that's leaping ahead) I adopted a logo for the extricate's journey I had already begun planning, the end to a decades-long career in New York City mainstream publishing, and continued making my way north.

Actual rabbit holes and Andre's trees included, images of nature have always figured heavily in how, if not where, I have lived. Despite fifty-plus years' residence in the various boroughs of New York City, it is nature that has provided my symbols and my signals. Field guides and back-to-the-land classics such as a 1940 edition of M. G. Kains's *Five Acres and Independence* or *Living the Good Life* (Helen and Scott Nearing, 1954) have filled my bookshelves, fueling my fantasy life of longing to just *get the hell out of here.* Even the most obscure bits of bird behavior or meteorological patterns hold a magnetism for me, as do little-known phenomena like diapause—a stunning survival mechanism in insects that can be invoked in the face of danger—and other such tactics for not getting swallowed up.

When I left the safety zone, I wagered big that nature would continue to show me the way, if only I stayed quiet enough to be able to hear the bird sing (and the snake—or the seeds inside a dried gourd, still alive and wanting out of an increasingly brittle shell before it's too late—*rattle*). If only I would let the garden, and the bigger ecosystem it is tucked into, teach me.

For peace comes dropping slow, William Butler Yeats wrote after the line of "The Lake Isle of Innisfree" that is this book's title. Finding peace, and even making it, yes, and also metamorphosis can be time-consuming undertakings. I have already learned this from my backyard friends the green frogs, who wait as long as twenty-two months—holding on, half-baked, even through a hard winter, before letting go of their heavy, unneeded, but familiar tails. The guides are all around me—human, plant, animal, even what for lack of another explanation I must call spirits—offering to help flesh out *My Story of Me*, which I hope proves a myth that I can live with the rest of my days. Some are familiar voices—the same lifetime-long messengers whose tip-offs I pretended not to hear when they spoke the first (second, third...) time, back in the old country. *Can't you see I'm in a meeting?* I'd say in a shrill voice heard only inside my head. *Not now, not now.* These days, utterances of messengers old and new are all playing involuntarily on some weird tape-delay, playing loud through every speaker in my universe; spewing out at me over the wi-fi radio, in my dreams, everywhere.

Attention, attention! the Zen master teaches. I've got a lot of listening to do.

SOME OF MY EARLIEST NEW-WORLD RUMINATIONS took the form of blogging—posting old and new personal garden writing on an impromptu site I created to homeschool myself in the do-it-yourself web, though mostly I "studied" after a glass of wine or two, and definitely without any business plan on file. I had run marthastewart.com in its early years, but now my kingdom was infinitely smaller, with me in every role—including the name on the URL. *Thank you, Jesus.* Chief Everything Officer: CEO at last.

But in the midst of all this important "work," the phone calls and e-mail inquiries started. *Can I come see what you're doing?*

You want to see my closets without so many jeans, my stacking toys? I am thinking, suddenly fully awake. *Attention!*

But come they all did, to Copake Falls, New York, and then

came the newspaper stories, the radio interviews, a national television appearance.

"This woman was living my dream—and the dream of so many other 50-somethings like us, who long to rekindle the creative fire that is snuffed out in the corporate world," Anne Raver wrote in the *New York Times* on June 19, 2008, two months after I launched my homemade hobby project, the blog called A Way to Garden.

By late summer, Adrian Higgins, a longtime *Washington Post* columnist, had made the pilgrimage, too. He drove nearly eight hours to see me, a stranger. Over and again that afternoon, and afterward in e-mails, his synopsis: "I am so envious that you had the nerve." Adrian's story appeared on September 11, 2008, seven years after the day that he correctly inferred was the true catalyst for all of what is happening now to me, and also probably popped the lid off a reservoir of yearning I heard in all those whose dream, I'm told, I am living.

From twenty- and thirty-something bloggers, to the head of the large group of NPR affiliates, who ran a three-part interview, the consensus those first months: Margaret Roach is onto something. She is on the path. *I've gotta get me some of that.* More than a thousand blog commenters, and hundreds of cold-call e-mailers, echoed the same thing: *Way to go, Margaret.* A Beatles refrain keeps echoing in my head: *Say the word, and you'll be free / Say the word and be like me.*

Like I said: Watch out; this might be contagious.

But I was surely an accidental touchstone, a trigger for their confessions about what predatory danger they, too, so want to elude; what depth of precious, lifesaving peace and quiet they want to achieve. So what is this dream of which they—perhaps you?—speak so longingly?

Have I in fact hit the jackpot?

(Do you believe in magic?)

True story:

As I sat down to write the proposal that would become this book—on the morning of July 13, 2008, six months into my post-Martha, post-paycheck life—an e-mail showed up in my in-box. It was the kind with a generic-enough sender so that you're not sure if it's spam or for real. I opened it.

Hey, I'd been purchasing lottery tickets down at the Xtra-Mart, so why not open an e-mail? The body of that message:

Twenty years from now you will be more disappointed by the things you didn't do than by the ones you did do. So throw off the bow-lines. Sail away from the safe harbor. Catch the trade winds in your sails. Explore. Dream. Discover.   —Mark Twain

The e-mail was in fact spam, but it certainly was intended for me. The spammer in this case was an idiot savant, and I am grateful.

Be grateful to everyone, the ancient sage Atisha taught, and that means everyone: those on your favorites list, and those on your shit list, too. Not just beings who approach you laden with gifts, but ones who bring you their burdens and pass you their hot potatoes. Be grateful even if they try to scare you away with venomous behavior.

True story:

Two weeks after the Mark Twain fortune-cookie-ish e-mail,

as Month 8 of my adventure began, I was really gaining on it. I was getting properly dressed in street clothes most days, and only occasionally waking up that way. Progress, unless you count the number of mornings I awoke parallel to the headboard, my head to the west and feet to the east instead of the south-north direction I'd started in. *(Note to self: Tell shrink, but don't dwell on such minor details.)*

I was especially proud that I'd honored one of the trickier commitments I'd made to myself when I left the city: to work at preventing complete social isolation. It was a legitimate fear—more to those who care about me than in my own mind, however—after more than thirty years of working long hours in the lively community inherent in any corporate environment, and particularly because I am in many ways a solitary type. Work had been my village and family. Despite my recent rural reclusion, though, I had made two new friends, and was going to see one of them for dinner.

It was a Friday night, exactly seven fifteen. Hair done, makeup and even some jewelry on—baubles I hadn't worn since my exodus. A bottle of smartly chosen red was stashed in my bag for my oenophile hosts, a successful Hollywood screenwriter and his ex-Yalie wife, whom I'd met (magic?) because she was one of my blog's first commenters; they are likewise recent refugees from urban living. Perfect.

Perfect? I should have known better *(with a girl like you . . .)*. It was the first day in the first month in my entire adult life that I had no paycheck to cash. The day had already included a total solar eclipse and a series of biblical electrical storms, the kind my first country months had been unnervingly loaded with, the kind I'd weathered beneath the 1877 Swedish dining table or huddled inside the enclosed staircase, shaking.

I don't think that there is anything that is really magical unless it has a terrifying quality, said the painter Andrew Wyeth. The storm's passing had seemed to clear the air, to change the charge of things, and I was feeling exhilarated, enthusiastic, open. I was going out. New friends had been delivered, cause for celebration.

I shut the inner door and swung the screen out then quickly back behind me, too, as I stepped my left foot onto the black rubber doormat.

The longest journey begins with a single step, and this was definitely the one, landing me right in the path of a five-foot-long timber rattlesnake, the well-named *Crotalus horridus*. No; I did not burst into an impromptu David Byrne lyric just then, but if this tale should become a musical: *We caught a rattlesnake, now we've got something for dinner. / We got it. We got it.*

Technically, all my shelves of field guides remind me, as a Homo sapiens I am this animal's predator. It felt distinctly the other way around.

Note to readers: An *Eat, Pray, Love*–style pilgrimage to India is not a requirement for those seeking (rude) awakening. And apparently the package I'd selected for my enlightenment tour was the all-inclusive, deluxe one—close encounter with large, venomous reptile included.

I suffer from a lifelong case of ophidiophobia: a fear and loathing of those (including snakes) who slither through their lives, and periodically shed their skins. With regularity in adulthood, I have been visited by snake dreams at night. During every period of personal upheaval, I have been visited by snakes during waking hours, too: snakes in my living room; curled on the kitchen windowsill between the screen and inner window I was opening; on the bathroom floor waiting for me beside the toilet when I got up in the darkness from a long-ago boyfriend's bed, a bed I didn't really want to be in, anyhow.

Try as I might, I hadn't quite taken in the advice of the great New York State naturalist John Burroughs, advice based on his own observations in the woods just across the Hudson River from here at the start of the twentieth century:

The lesson which life repeats and constantly reinforces is "look under foot." You are always nearer the divine and the true sources of your power than you think.

Me? I scream. And then in midshriek, I rush away. I try not to look—though with a venomous snake you must look, and keep on looking, if there is to be any hope of catching and relocating it a short distance away from the house. I know the drill: I must somehow watch the snake and also grab the phone and call for help in the form of the nearest person who has both the license and gear to accomplish this sensitive measure. On that July evening, I had lost sight of the snake by the time that help arrived.

For a serious gardener, fear of snakes is a liability. For a serious gardener in one of the remaining northeastern habitats of a threatened or endangered American pit viper, it has required a constant test of that fear (or courage). In more than twenty years of weekends spent rooting around on my piece of land, though, I had never encountered *Crotalus horridus*. Not here; on the road, yes, and in the woods, but not here. The timber rattler is well known to all the other settlers scattered sparsely along this dirt byway cut into the midslope of a steep, fourteen-hundred-foot hillside, but did not show himself to me until that night. Perhaps he knew I had not been prepared, and kindly waited to come calling at the kitchen door until I seemed to be all good and settled in.

Welcome to your new life, Margaret. Was that what he was saying when he rose up and shook his stack of rattles? Or perhaps, *Don't tread on me*, the meaning assigned to the rattlesnake's image on pre-Revolutionary flags, a cry against oppression, a signal of readiness to strike against those who would deny his freedom.

Or, *I am here, Margaret, and watching, even when you don't see me. I'm waiting for you to take it all off. Come on, silly girl; it's not so damn hard. Shed.*

True story:

Late summer arrived, and though I would not be going "back to school" full-time that fall, I had a meeting in the city the week of Labor Day.

I went in the night before to have supper with my closest friend and garden mentor, Marco, at his home in the Bronx, where I still kept a rental place. Arriving a bit ahead of our scheduled dinner hour, I dropped my bag and washed up before going five houses down the block. On the stretch of grass between my parking space and the front door, a distance of perhaps twenty-five feet that I had tread on thousands of times in more than a decade—*going to the office; returning from the office; going to the office; returning from the office*—I noticed something by my left foot, the foot that I'd presented just weeks before to that timber rattler.

This is the Bronx, mind you, but I have almost stepped on a discarded snakeskin. I do not know what generous creature left it, but I have no doubt that it was put there for me. I keep it now in a ziplock bag on my bulletin board, in case I should ever think I have been imagining things.

"How'm I doing?" as New York City Mayor Ed Koch used to say. "You know how I always ask everybody how am I doing?" he is quoted in the 1981 book named for his most famous interrogative. "Well, today I asked myself, and the answer was, 'Terrific.'"

Terrific (from the Latin word for frighten, incidentally), yes, but let's be honest: I live with a cat, and an independent, disinterested one at that, a stray male who adopted me the morning of September 11, 2001, when I pulled into my weekend country driveway at twelve twenty PM from Manhattan, a cat who mostly inhabited a small building behind my house by mutual consent. Sort of our version of separate bedrooms.

I am childless. And parentless. I have no reliable income, and I have not managed to really scale back anywhere near far enough. I applied for unemployment insurance in that first July and got turned down because of a technicality that backfired; I had incorporated my new life, in anticipation of doing ongoing consulting and other work (the work that has all just dried up).

The world's "credit tsunami," a "hundred-year event," unfolded in increasingly sickening chapters as an insistent backdrop to my own much smaller monetary wonderings. And I repeat: On the first day of the first month in my adult life that went unsalaried, just hours after a total solar eclipse, I stepped out my door onto a giant rattlesnake.

Then why was everybody (including the reptile) still giving me the high five?

Apparently these kind strangers were, as I had been, feeling trapped. (Sound familiar yet?) So strong was their projection that they attributed my new life with characteristics it doesn't even have: They perceived my glass those first months as not just half full, but positively brimming over. Craving optimism about the second "half" of life, they imagine it can all work out—if only they, too, can break free and find refuge, or at least *la diritta via*.

> *Nel mezzo del cammin di nostra vita*
> *mi retrovai per una selva oscura,*
> *che la diritta via era smarrita.*
> *(In the middle of the journey of our life*
> *I found myself in a dark wood,*
> *for the straight way was lost.)*

—DANTE, *THE DIVINE COMEDY*

In fact all that happened those first months here in the woods, besides some serious bouts of cleaning, is that everything I fear was being systematically delivered to my doorstep, as if to say: *And this: Deal with this, too, please, Margaret. Now.*

Would an appropriate man be delivered next?

The next special delivery that first summer was my ex-husband, whom I had not seen in more than fifteen years and who, basically, has loathed me most of that time because of my one-sided decision twentyish years ago to leave our marriage. I plead temporary insanity, or at least total exhaustion; we had married in the wake of my mother's moving into full-time care for her early-onset Alzheimer's, a disease that visited her before she was fifty and brought me home to oversee her for several unspeakably ugly years in the house I was raised in.

Then, maybe a year into our marriage—and weeks before I left it—I nursed my best friend to his own dementia and death from AIDS. There was nothing left for me to share—nothing to have or to hold on the bare nubbin I had become.

The day my ex simply appeared unannounced in the driveway here, apparently on an impulsive detour en route to his oldest friend's home nearby, I had been out mowing. I did not love the moment of recognition then—an awkward sentence or two of explaining I was now here full-time and his explaining, in turn, what brought him to the neighborhood—and then as quick as he came, he was gone. But I cherish the image now, the mental snapshot of our reunion: I was heading back down the road to the barn on my beloved orange tractor, wearing my ersatz pajamas and a hoodie as old as the Gap itself and safety goggles and giant noise-reduction earmuffs, when I saw the unfamiliar red 1949 pickup parked across the end of my driveway. He did not recognize me, or at least not at first. Who would have?

Apparently, provocative events like global economic crises bring out all manner of ghosts along with the varmints, and not just from Wall Street or out from under rocks.

Be grateful to everyone.

There have, thankfully, been more agreeable visits by gentlemen callers.

On April 19, 2008, three weeks into my aimless garden blogging, I wrote this entry after holding a camera in my left hand to photograph a frog who was in my right one:

My, my how times have changed. Four months ago I was wearing designer clothes and living in fluorescent light. Today I was mucking out water gardens in the sun, and refitting plumbing gaskets while my boyfriends looked on disinterestedly. All nine of them (all just like this hunk I'm about to grab). Handsome, huh? Heaven, huh?

It had taken me exactly a year to position myself within reach of the princely bullfrog, and this new life stage; a year of negotiating the contractual timing and terms of my Martha departure, and of planning my escape. Those old journals—the ones I had the time and drive to look at in the first months upstate—reveal I'd actually been planning my departure actively for more than seven years, since the year 2000.

On the way "home," I had seen every manner of therapist and adviser (physical and psychiatric, financial, legal, astrological), started buying the weekly lottery tickets, and cleaned every corner of my life out to lighten the load I had to carry to the New World. I had hired the professional matchmaker, writing a giant check despite my disappeared income, wanting to head regret off at the pass by ensuring I didn't let happily ever after elude me if money could, in fact, buy you love. Bases covered. *Check.*

On the eve of the *New York Times* story, I even gave one of my closest friends, an ex-boyfriend whom I treasured and somehow hoped would mend his ways, the heave-ho. I was going to cross this threshold unencumbered, without Martha, without Max Mara, without him. Without all those jeans. With all my plastic lids, at least, fitted on right.

Eradication, extirpation—and even evisceration. *Out, out damn spot!* There were a few additions, a couple of high-ticket items I brought into my new life, like better bird-watching binoculars and a serious wi-fi radio to keep me company. But perhaps most notably among my tax receipts for this first year of self-employed stillness was one for twenty dollars spent at Staples, a New Year's binge. The booty: a bulletin board, pushpins, and index cards.

The intention: to post (without applying judgment or editing) any and all ideas—to just allow and witness them. The board, cards, and pins were my "twenty dollars to a new life kit," and I more than got my money's worth. My own lid was coming off now, and each card was a fumarole, venting built-up steam. The crazy collage included cards with lines from songs I'd grabbed from the wi-fi stream, diced from tunes the DJ seemed to be spinning just for me:

I feel so close to everything we've lost. (Sincerely, L. Cohen.)

Gonna rise up, find my direction magnetically. Gonna rise up, throw out my ace in the hole. (Good advice, Eddie Vedder.)

Bold as love. (Thank you, Jimi.)

We ain't going to hell. We're going to the rebel side of heaven. (How'd you know, Langhorne Slim?)

Cards with questions to myself, including that trickiest, loudest one: *Who are you in a digital age, if you are not mroach@ marthastewart dot com anymore?*

Cards with titles of projects I imagined at some moment or other that I might undertake: *Story of woman who communicates with lovers solely in iTunes playlists, having given up on "talking things over."*

On another set of cards, I also (bravely?) had written a fear list:

Snakes.

Electrical storms and power outages.

Airplanes.

Dying alone.

(And not necessarily in that order.)

Right off I started making more progress facing my fear list than anything on the other cards, all the while hoping the last entry needn't be encountered anytime soon (and particularly not as a result of a bite by Item Number 1). Dare we put a collective foot across the threshold and see what actually unfolded? First we will need to go backward to look forward, though—a lesson I am increasingly learning—to where my hunger and my restlessness began.

Chapter 2

The Directions to Here

Come on over to my yard
Sit around
And let your troubles all disappear
Come on over to my yard
'Cause right now heaven's right here.

—JEB LOY NICHOLS, "HEAVEN RIGHT HERE"

How did I go from She Who Lives in the World to She Who Lives in the Woods, navigating a slow route between the West Side Highway and Valley View Road, where instead of potholes, ruts deeper than the wheel wells shape up to punctuate multiple mud seasons each year?

I knew at once that I would perch myself here, on this steep but not rocky bit of north-facing slope above that dirt road. I knew the day I saw the little house twenty-one years before, but it took every bit of those two decades to arrive, or even really begin arriving in the sense of the total surrender I think I always had in mind somewhere—hidden deep, perhaps, but there.

I know we met on a sunny day, the house and I, because I still have the one photograph of it that I took then. It is an image of the previous owners hurriedly bending to tasks out front on that early summer day because *someone was coming.* They are captured on Kodachrome as they stooped and knelt, engulfed in unmown lawn beside a little white shoe box that had way too long needed painting. I wouldn't know it bore even deeper signs of neglect until later in our relationship.

They were, as I would become, weekenders from the city, and you could see the wear and tear of it on them and the place. The country does not wait to do its wild things just because you have not pulled into the driveway yet; it doesn't wait for Friday evenings, or cease on Sundays at five o'clock. It perpetrates them behind your back, a naughty friend who always has a trick or several in store, or on the better Fridays not a trick at all but some indescribably delicious handiwork: a lipstick sunset; the billowing lavender-colored bloom of dame's rocket along the shady roadsides flanking your approach; several baby birds in the tiniest nest on the ledge where you keep the spare key. *Surprise!*

You never know which side of its personality the country will be showing, though, until you have arrived.

The house was not charming; it is hard to be charming when all your character has been wrapped in layers of falseness, layers of what is not you but rather brands burned into your surface and even deeper at someone else's convenience or desire.

It was love at first sight. We were each other's intended, no denying it.

But the solitary photo, a cheap drugstore print now curled at the edges that I keep in an album in an old Chinese cupboard in the living room, tells the story of what had been perpetrated on the tiny building. Its footprint is just six hundred square feet, the simplest of two-story structures that amounted to no more (scalewise) than a box of twenty tea bags standing on its long side, with a steep-pitched roof up top. It's called an I-house in the architectural language of simple buildings; because it lacks any wings or embellishments, from a bird's-eye view, you'd just see the shape of the letter *I*. As if not plain and quiet enough, the poor little building had been muffled and disguised, a gag order on whatever little bit of personality it might have had at birth in the mid-1880s long suffocated beneath another layer of siding, and maybe one more for good measure. Character assassination.

Except for one thing: that vergeboard, the big piece of gingerbread hanging in the gable end high above the front door, a feature layered onto even the simplest of Victorian homes, as if to say: *We're somebody, too.* Everything else the house might have had going for it: gone, hidden under one-too-many layers of siding that a series of previous owners had found easier and probably cheaper solutions to a century or so of pest damage or paint prep. The little house was wrapped in so much siding that there was no reveal remaining to its window trim—it was flush (and not in the best sense of that word at all).

You have seen houses like that, or perhaps you live in one, as I did on weekends for twenty years. I always ache for them; I want to park a Dumpster in their driveways and peel off all of that burden.

On the inside of my house-to-be, more disguises had been imposed with insensitive or at least impatient hands. The same one-dimensionality where walls met windows was accomplished when (instead of gutting first, or replastering) three-eighths-inch Sheetrock and a layer of Masonite had been nailed into place over crumbly plaster, with the added insult of a range of floral-patterned vinyl wallpapers layered over that.

Since the interior walls and window trim were now a level surface, achieving unintended and equally unfortunate symmetry with the house's exterior, the vinyl flowers-by-the-roll simply went right over the molding to the window openings, and even around the bend quite literally on some open doorways. Seeking an alternative to scraping and painting your trim? *Wallpaper it, baby; let 'er roll.*

I am left with other indelible first impressions: lime green shag carpet in the living room; an Astroturf look-alike up the steep, narrow old enclosed staircase; stick-on plastic "bricks" (speaking of look-alikes) over the central chimney affixed in lieu of repointing. A bathtub the size of a car, in a room (adjacent to the kitchen) the size of a very slightly larger car. Impossible—and mine, all mine.

But the house, *my house*, had me at vergeboard: It was a little house that screamed, and that fancy fretwork was the one bit that nobody could cover up. *Can you see me?* it seemed to say. *Can you see who I am in here, despite what they have done to me?*

Yes, of course I can, dearest; lopsided me of the extra earring hole in one lobe. Me of the mangy red blessing cord tied round my throat by a Tibetan nun or monk at some retreat, or mala beads or something else of that hippie sort always poking out from the neckline of the mid-tier Calvin Klein I had in that early-to-mid-career timeline halfheartedly surrendered to, en route to the Max Mara and Issey Miyake days that would eventually come. *I dare you to notice my defiance, world.* See, it's right here: right up top.

We met, my house and I, that day when I showed up so unexpectedly, before it could even tidy itself up a bit and be officially "on the market," and we quickly fell in love. How did I go from She Who Lives in the World to She Who Lives in the Woods? I blame the power of the sad little house, which is where my life's detour began, or at least had its first conscious expressions. And then I suppose I spent twenty years systematically stripping off the muffling layers, the house's and mine, picking away and peeling, before it was finally ready for me and I for it—before the full reveals.

The French have a phrase for such first meetings as I had with my house: *coup de foudre*, or clap of thunder. Psychiatrists must have a phrase, too, but it is probably not as poetic, something about being attracted to the wrong characters or caretaking or some such, about being the patron saint of lost causes.

Yes, I always like an underdog, preferably one with lots of costly quirks.

But it was with that clap of thunder that my house and I began an extended long-distance relationship, able to see each other only a couple of days a week for twenty years, but happy for every reunion. It was in that resounding moment that I glimpsed my future—a phrase I'd up till then thought was reserved for career or marital planning. No, the sorry little house was my future; I just did not quite grasp that fully yet.

IT WAS THE MAN IN THE RED TRUCK who became my first neighbor, in the true sense of the word. Not someone who lives next door, because there is no such person; the little house is contiguous to thousands of acres of farms and Taconic State Park land, mostly wooded, but in the jungle-like second-growth way, onetime farm fields gone back to a tangle of stunted, strangled weed trees and vines thick as my waist. My two-plus acres float like the tiniest island in an oceanic semiwilderness, and so when we speak of neighbors here it is not a matter of physical proximity as much as commitment, and of reliable kindness.

The man in the red truck (a farmer, I quickly deduced, since his end of the road was dotted with the traditional long red buildings of dairy farms) was kind to me from the very start of our relationship, and in him I found a kindred spirit who has remained a blessing these two-plus decades.

My editor will be tempted to take this next bit out, as it is too conveniently perfect, the way those fabricated parts in headlinegrabbing memoirs are, but it is true: As if to help make mine a good story, as if to cast this book before I even thought of writing it and also the Hallmark Hall of Fame television movie, the man in the red truck turned out to be named Herb; his wife is Flora (and no, good people that they are, they did not name their five children things like Poppy and Dahlia, though there is a junior Herb). In time Herb's Flora would teach me to can and pickle and make jam—how to be a perfect country housewife.

But I did not know him by his name those first months; I knew him only by his passages up and down the road. I knew him by his sound, the distinctive creaking of the fencelike panels that enclosed the vehicle's bed, rubbing loudly in their slots as the truck negotiated the inevitable ruts out front. Sound bounces off the rocky, iron ore–filled ridge behind me, funneled from one end of the road to the other in a perfect demonstration of wave theory. In the tremendous quiet of the place, you hear everything before you see it.

My portion of our road, as everyone on it likes to mention, is the worst stretch of all; the bumpiest and most unstable. Right in front of my house is where the difficulties in navigation always begin, where things get noisy.

I took ownership of the little house in the autumn of 1986, drawing my boyfriend (the one I would marry briefly, later) into the adventure, into the back-to-the-land make-believe, with me. We quickly set to clearing up the neglected place of derelict trees and countless brambles that always look at unmown acreage as prime opportunities for a campaign of Manifest Destiny and not so gradually turn field back into forest, one insistent and often prickly woody shoot at a time.

I soon learned the mastery of several tools: a weed whip but with a star blade attached instead of heavy nylon filament, not unlike having a whirring chop saw or a giant, spinning X-shaped razor blade at the end of a long arm; a mattock, sort of a pickax but with a chisel-like blade well suited to the toughest digging; a pry bar for wrestling out the knobby and persistent roots of the *Rubus* once sawn down and partly dislodged; a giant lopper for severing any roots that remained. Oh, and very serious reinforced leather boots and gloves in case any of the above missed their mark. Don't forget your safety goggles.

This was nasty work, thorny and endless and therefore one of rural living's best metaphors, and the defeated brambles and felled dead trees had to be dragged off to an open area where we assembled what would be our first burn pile. (If you think you want to live in the country, start by clearing a thicket of brambles, invasive woody vines, and choked, decaying trees, and then decide. This or its equivalent will basically become your life practice. There are always thorny bits in your path, always.)

Back and forth those first autumn months of my part-time residence the man in the red truck would go, raising a hand as if to say hello, but in that way that the Queen raises hers: more a formality than an act of full engagement, a gesture I'd soon come to learn was not royal at all but just what we did here, how we communicated when we were just passing by, noninvasive but observant. He'd wave in that requisite manner, like the gentleman who tipped his hat for ladies back in the day, all the while watching us as our pile of trimmings grew.

I suspect he knew from the day we heaped up the first branches and logs that an intervention was ahead, but in the most neighborly of manners he just watched as we convicted ourselves of repeat acts of gross naïveté.

And then one afternoon the man could stall the inevitable no longer: Two city kids and a brush pile as big as a one-car garage, a mass that would not light, proved irresistible incitement. Even the man in the red truck could not remain silent on the matter. He passed by, heading noisily in the direction of his home, and shortly afterward the creaking, bouncing sound of that old dump truck with its weary springs and loose side panels returned, slowed, and stopped. Stopped.

Out he climbed, maneuvering down to ground level from on high, really arriving, an entrance. And over to the pile, and to us, he walked in the manner I have since come to know as distinctly his: purposeful but never rushed, a man going somewhere but also content to take his time getting there.

"Having trouble getting that to go?" the man in the red truck said, in case perhaps we hadn't noticed, stating the obvious but without a hint of sneering. The man in the red truck is nothing if not matter-of-fact in all matters.

"That won't work," he then said, pointing at the measly piles of newspaper and cardboard we'd been using as igniter, behaving as if we were bending to the simpler task of making a fire from well-seasoned wood in the controlled environment of a fireplace.

From that first gesture, I was struck and taken in by his capability. The man in the red truck had these enormous forearms—evidence, he would happily reveal at the slightest provocation, of a youth spent at least in part behind a jackhammer on tunnel-building projects in New England to earn money, and playing minor-league baseball.

"You'll need an old tire," he said, and pointed to the truck. "I have one if you want it." He'd come prepared.

Let me quickly say that we have all since learned the environmental unsoundness of this practice, of stuffing a tire with newspaper, tucking it into your brush pile, and using it as a fire starter, but twenty-five years ago it was regarded as wisdom: a form of recycling, a way that farmers here and everywhere kept their fields clear of woody invasion and used up worn tires from farm vehicles—ones not needed to weigh down the silage-covering tarps or for some other critical duty—in the process. I was in awe.

That clap of fire, *coup de feu*, would bind me to Herb until one of us goes first, and even after that. You do not soon, or ever, forget the person who imparts the secret of fire.

The pile burned for several days, the last day without flames but instead a giant bed of white-hot coals that in the darkness overnight seemed to inhale and exhale, glowing red-orange and then less so with each pulse of its breath. Eventually, it was just ash and the steel belts from that steel-belted radial—strange circles of wire I'd never known the exact meaning of—but nothing more remained.

No trace, is how Zen master Shunryu Suzuki described it. *When you do something, you should burn yourself completely, like a good bonfire, leaving no trace of yourself.*

No trace but this: We stank of smoke; our clothes were saturated with the odor. But we were proud to hold the secret of fire—flatlanders (as those from elsewhere are referred to in New England) who had passed the first rite, if barely.

The tire that started it was the first token of our friendship, Herb's and mine, but it would not be the last treasure he would haul out of that truck or another of his trucks to follow, to show me what I'd need to know to get by on the road that would really connect us as proper neighbors from that day on.

THE MEETING WITH HERB WAS MORE THAN JUST a lesson learned or handed down. With the start of that friendship came the start of something else: the realization of my powerlessness and near ignorance of all things country.

Take, for instance, the fact that I didn't even really know where I was.

Yes, of course I had a map; I had found and bought the place, hadn't I? But where I really was eluded me for some time to come. You know how maps are: One's of a state, another's of a county, as if nothing more exists than the material promised on the front panel: Map of New York State, Map of Columbia County. Even within an atlas, a whole book of maps, it's each to its own page, the boundaries observed. My first months or maybe years part-time in the country in the 1980s were just like that: I stayed within the lines, kept to my own page.

Silly girl didn't think to ask what was past the right-hand margin of the county map I studied each weekend to try to jump-start an intimacy with the area that I had never even heard of, despite growing up just downstate from it, a distance of less than 150 miles.

I read history, at first, if not geography, though; learned that Columbia County was rich in the heritage of Henry Hudson (its seat is named for him), and that it's roughly *Last of the Mohicans* land. I learned from a piece of slippery, gleaming slag glass (like a shard of a giant marble unearthed while gardening) and from the curiosity that this blue rock so unlike any other elicited in me that my hamlet had once been named Copake Iron Works. Slag, which I still turn up here and there on my piece of ground, an unexpected jewel in the crown of the ever-generous soil, is a waste product of the smelting of iron ore. The abandoned furnaces are just a three-minute walk in the woods beyond my house; the former mine, or pit, like another down the road apiece in the opposite direction, has since flooded and been turned into a swimming feature of the state park it belongs to today.

In 1845, when Copake Iron Works was founded as part of the larger and much older Town of Copake, there were no houses; by 1880, around the time that mine was built, there were forty, housing two hundred citizens, and three churches (two of which remain as active parishes). I have never been a churchgoer, but it is hard to resist the tiny, sharply pointed Gothic-style Episcopal church up on a knoll whose name—St. John in the Wilderness—speaks to what it was like here in 1852, at its founding, and still feels like to me, at least spiritually, these first dropout months. I love that it was St. John to whom the Book of Revelation is attributed; that John is following a mandate (presumably from Jesus), to *write the things which thou hast seen, and the things which are, and the things which shall be hereafter.*

The former railroad depot is now a small store, mostly serving park visitors in want of soda or snacks. It sits at the end of the paved recreational "rail-trail," once an active rail bed that stretched to New York City. Seven hundred fifty tons of quality iron a year left that depot annually; now only bicycles and pedestrians do, most of them weekend visitors like I once was.

So engrossed was I in fixing the house and making a garden at first that I remained long ignorant of the fact that the Berkshire Mountains of Massachusetts and the Litchfield Hills of Connecticut are just across the hillside, as close or closer than the only town of size in my own county and much more developed. And I was ignorant, too, of many other neighbors and realities bigger than myself—none of them shy—who would all show themselves in due course.

I was oblivious to being in rattlesnake country, or that a two-hundred-foot waterfall was just up the hill (Massachusetts's largest, and right on that state border that I didn't know was almost literally in my backyard); oblivious of living in a nearly all-Republican stronghold (a lesson I learned on primary day that very first fall at the Grange Hall, because I have voted here from the start); ignorant of the ferocity of electrical storms and other feats of meteorology that would soon send their greetings, a strange and staggered set of welcome wagons, I suppose. I managed to be unaware for some time that I had come to live with not just deer (which as a gardener I came here already sensitized to) but also bears, mountain lions, bobcats, coyotes, gray and red foxes, possums, porcupines, rabbits, raccoons, skunks, beavers, weasels, woodchucks, three species of squirrels, chipmunks, and every other rodent and insectivore from moles to shrews to bats—and undoubtedly some creatures I am now forgetting even though by this time we have all definitely met. All of these creatures call the place theirs, often as I lay sleeping—and each one knows it better by far than I.

Taken in by my own conjured fantasy of *Little House in the Big Woods*, I was also astonishingly oblivious to matters of the interior landscape: mine, and that of humankind in general. Blithe spirit was I, particularly to the fact of how any change that is begun (whether voluntarily, as in this case, or ones that happen to you) lands us smack onto a threshold, a place of neither-here-nor-thereness; duration and outcome indeterminate. It proved much easier and faster to strip away layers of wallpaper and wallboard and to turn increasingly large swaths of sod under into the soil, fixing up my fixer-upper and creating garden beds where grass once grew, than to strip away attachment to self-esteem, income, and the increasing carrot of career advancement. Turning a crumbly white house the color green and also somewhat sturdier, and a semijungle into a yard and then eventually a garden and even a landscape, was no match for what it took to turn Margaret brave enough to live among the locals of all descriptions. Much as I dreamed and pretended I belonged here—invoking the getaway fantasy when urban reality was all too much—it would take years and also something profound to shove me off the doorstep into this full-time.

Madwoman in a Mad World

EVERYONE HAS A 9/11 STORY; in my end-of-boomer generation or older, it's stored in that corner of the mind with *Where were you when Kennedy was shot?* (at PS 94 in Little Neck, New York; we were rounded up and taken to the basement lunchroom, where all the teachers were crying), and with *Where were you when James Earl Ray killed Martin Luther King Jr.?* (with Eva, our black housekeeper, in my parents' bedroom; Eva was ironing, and we'd just been watching a game show or *The 4:30 Movie* on the television, I think, when the news broke in and she began to weep).

When the first plane struck the towers I was coming upstairs from the garage of the Starrett-Lehigh Building, on West 26th Street and the Hudson River in Manhattan, having parked my car as I did each morning on my way to Martha Stewart's Internet and e-commerce headquarters. The way that landmark, block-square building, a former industrial and warehouse facility, is built, and why it was built, made all the difference in my experience of that day of days.

Starrett-Lehigh was erected to take advantage of its waterfront access, its purpose to receive freight unloaded from the piers across from it as cargo ships came in. And it was a gleaming masterpiece of modernist industrial design: From the unbroken run of twenty-pane steel-sash windows that wrap the wedding cake–like tiered structure, you can see the Statue of Liberty. You could see the Twin Towers. You could see everything, unobstructed.

"A small plane just hit the Trade Center," the receptionist said, standing at the wall of windows, her back uncharacteristically facing the entry doors and front desk, as I came off the elevator at eight fifty for my nine o'clock meeting.

I was the senior officer of this facility, one of three locations the company had then, so I hurried to find a working radio or television and also to locate another executive I knew would be there that day, our CFO. Jim was in an interior office, and when I found him, still unaware. We went to the south-facing wall of windows together, and then it happened: At 9:03, the second plane seemed from our confusing vantage point on that eerily bright day to turn, then hit the second tower.

"Thousands of people just died," I said to Jim in a reflex to the witnessed impact, and then suggested we evacuate everyone down the emergency staircase and get them home, fast.

Up and down each row of desks on the 175,000-square-foot floor we moved systematically, quickly gathering people to help spread the word: *Go home.* And once they were out and dispersing, I fled, too: into my car, parked down in the building's garage, and up the West Side Highway, clearing the bridge even before the city was locked down. That's how fast I went from the sight of the second impact to out of there: I beat the bridge and tunnel lockdown.

I stopped that morning near my city rental place, just north of Manhattan in the Riverdale section of the Bronx, hoping to find refuge with my closest male friend and neighbor at his workplace at the public garden called Wave Hill, just across from where we each lived. Marco, with his staff of gardeners, was in the potting shed, listening to the news, and like everyone in a fast-widening circle of awareness, trying to grasp the confusing, impossible details.

The garden and even the company of this treasured friend

proved no refuge, though; no perceived safe house. By just before ten thirty, when the second tower collapsed, military helicopters were already buzzing the fly zone the Hudson River naturally provides, a route that Wave Hill, like the Twin Towers, was built to gaze out upon from on high. Frantic at the bulletins and the chopper noise and all of it, I said good-bye and hurried onward, farther north, as if there would be solace if I just kept running.

What there was instead was a large black cat, a cat I'd seen just once before but who was standing in the eerie, stunning sunlight of that day, who rolled delightedly in the warm driveway gravel of my weekend home and bared his belly as if we'd known each other for a lifetime, as if to say, *Welcome home.*

Our one previous meeting had been three months earlier, when in the middle of a birthday party I'd given for myself, a party with a boisterous group of forty-five margarita-filled adults spilling out into the yard in all directions from the tiny house, he'd apparently just walked in and shown himself to a real cat person in the group, who (a bit tipsy herself) had carried him inside to me.

I was at the stove, the oven door ajar, serving up still-hot shortcake biscuits with strawberries and cream at that very moment, engineering an assembly line of homemade dessert for nearly four dozen. There had just been a small mishap with the handheld electric beater, sending foamy cream-colored splatters everywhere, but people were holding out plates to get them filled, as if they didn't notice the spray of recently airborne cream on me, the wall, the appliances—or simply didn't care.

That was when I first met the black cat, and promptly asked

that Susan, the person presenting him to me in the midst of this drunken, whipped-cream chaos, please get him out of here.

I am, you see, not a cat person.

I am a bird person, and cats are a leading enemy of songbirds. After collisions with window glass, which is the top killer of songbirds in residential environments, cats rate next on the lethal list, killing hundreds of millions of birds a year in the United States alone, says the Audubon Society. I have spent my adulthood reading about and watching birds as a passionate amateur hobby, if not an obsession, and making a garden specifically geared to welcoming them year-round. I know better than to want a cat here with me, unless it was a cat who wanted to live indoors, a truly domesticated cat, the couch-and-bed type.

Did I mention how much I dislike pet hair on my floors and furniture and clothing?

This very large black and white male cat—a fur pattern for obvious reason referred to as tuxedo—being held out like a live offering in my direction from Susan's arms was that tricky mix of wild and tame that I'd known in too many men already (always ones carefully chosen for their low body-hair count, I might add, so that at least that one thing about them would not rankle me, or cause me extra work). *Get him out of here.*

Of course, he never did get out, but apparently kept an eye on me, gauging the right moment to make his next move toward his version of domestic bliss. He was christened Jack a few months hence, when he joined me for good the morning of September 11 and parked himself in a wooden box on the back porch, basking in the deceptive light and warmth of that darkest of mid-September days. "Jack in the Box," said Susan's longtime partner,

Harry, after she'd told him of coming back a few days later to find us—me, and this cat—still sitting out there with NPR playing on the boombox, trying to fathom the world's new landscape.

And so it was: Jack.

Be grateful to everyone.

At nearly sixteen pounds, the vet called Jack "big boned" when Susan took him in a week or two thereafter, and in fact he was not fat but wildly muscular, built like a miniature black panther and with all the moves, lowering himself to ground level and waiting, completely still, sometimes for half an hour until the very moment to positively race and then pounce upon his prey with shocking accuracy. Owing to his evolutionary ancestors, Jack sleeps most of the day and hunts at night. Fierce as he is, I should have named him Huey (for Newton) or Bobby (Seale), perhaps; he has certainly caused a revolution in my life. We also learned that he was about two years old, and had been neutered; probably, the vet said, a cat someone had not wanted anymore, a trade-in. Or maybe he had just grown sick of his old life and walked out one day.

It was Susan, who helps me in the garden and who in my city years was also the de facto caretaker here, whom Jack regarded as his owner, I think, at least at first, and to this day only Susan has ever done the vet appointments, tossing him into the pickup (no pet carrier or cage will ever know this cat) in the same madcap way she pulls him around on her tarp through the garden, a pile of trimmings or weeds and a heap of doglike Jack. She calls him Pum-kin, no *p* discernible in the middle. I call him something else: I call him Potentate. (Herb calls him Baby, speaking in baby talk when he does, and uses feminine pronouns to refer to the big black beast; I know not why, and do not ask.)

In our years together this animal, himself an offering I'd at first refused (*do not look a gift cat in the mouth?*) and then inadvertently adopted, has brought me many offerings. There have been mouse ass-ends, tail attached; mouse ass-ends, tail missing; mouse tails, no ass attached; moles and chipmunks, limp but outwardly undamaged (not good eating, apparently); young rabbits and possums, their spines slack, with portions of their fuselage missing; the distinctive furry tails of countless weasels (an animal I wish he didn't have such a taste for, as important as they are in keeping order in the native food chain); and so many parts whose origin was unknown—gizzardlike hard bits, occasional smears of whole intestines, and mostly just not-yet-quite-dried pools of red blood on my green back-porch floor. *Merry Christmas?* Did I fail to mention that I have been a vegetarian for more than thirty years?

And yes, of course, the marauding carnivore that is Jack had even delivered the occasional bird, and once or twice in the first years together, one of my beloved frogs.

We have not always done so well, wild man Jack and I, Jack the Demon Cat; there have been dark days between us, days when we did not speak. I was, after all, the Accidental Pet Owner, and (remember) not a cat person.

And he had been living in the woods before we dubbed him Jack. Alone in the woods.

"I heard that black cat who's been hanging around the woods is with you now," Deb, one half of the cat-loving couple who live a steep and rugged mile's distance up the adjacent road, said later that fall. News of my liaison, my broken resolve to live forever petless, had spread. People here have multiple serious pets with a purpose—barn cats, or mousers; dogs that hunt or retrieve fowl—and also farm animals. I had none, and was happy that way. "He was up here for a while," she said, "but then he disappeared, and we saw him darting in and out of the woods down by you all these last months. We wondered where he'd gone to lately."

When we pieced it together, it seems that apparently Jack-to-be had been fending for himself for probably half a year or longer, with three or more of those months spent watching me: the house with no animals, the place where he could maybe make a go of it. He had lived in a wild tangle of second-growth forest and adjacent field that is also the domain of bears and coyotes, bobcats and mountain lions—and to a lesser issue if you are a cat the size of Jack, of deer, gray and red foxes, possums and raccoons, porcupines and skunks, weasels and woodchucks, and every manner of smaller vertebrate and many species of snakes. He had lived on whatever moved and wasn't bigger or rougher or faster than he was.

And so from the glimpse on my birthday in June to the 9/11 morning in the driveway and into the wooden box out back, and then, before long, into a whole cottage of his own (a heated shed behind my house that became Jack's, cat door and all), before winter wrapped itself around us that year, my days with Jack began.

THE LONGEST JOURNEY BEGINS WITH A SINGLE CHECK. I used to make a lot of money, and as that expression you have heard (or said?) before serves to confess: The more I made, the more I spent.

I don't like to shop, to spend time in stores, strolling from one to another, trying things on; I never did. Malls make me physically ill, as do their parking lots. But I had become a heat-seeking binge shopper, walking up to Saks Fifth Avenue (which two other female executive Martha colleagues and I called "the 50th Street office") when things just got too hard. I could blow through five thousand dollars in fifteen or twenty minutes, a sort of *fuck-you-pay-me* reaction to whatever exercise in frustration the day had served up. The collection of designer work clothes that resulted from these "meetings" at Saks (sleekly underpinned with head-to-toe Wolford, of course; no mere Danskin or L'eggs for me) eventually gave way to a newfound interest in all manner of leather jackets.

For me it was never handbags or shoes, which held my two colleagues and most women I have known for emotional and economic ransom, but oh, those jackets. The good news: I only did this a few times a year (though with a ferocity that granted me a platinum Saks points card those years, the second-highest level of reward plan, and I might have hit diamond if I'd stuck around). The bad news: That behavior was nothing by comparison to how I acted out outdoors.

I survived the intensity of my "most successful" later corporate years by gardening on weekends with a vengeance (motivational Al Green CDs blaring on the boombox beside me), buying any plants I craved. And then I spent more money by hiring help for two of the days between my own visits—by hiring Susan, the ad hoc sponsor of Jack the cat—to care for the growing family. It had quickly exceeded the capability of even me, one exceptionally hyperactive weekender with no shortage of Monday-to-Friday issues to work out, and the highly effective long-handled round-point shovel I'd bought at a yard sale in the first upstate year decades back.

My coping mechanism, this gardening-frenzy-as-outlet, didn't work in winter, as USDA Zone 5B can drop as low as minus fifteen on average, and even the minus twenties. For four to five months a year, depending on what's dealt in that year's hand, there simply is no gardening allowed. The precious soil hides from me beneath a crusted-over moonscape fashioned from freeze-thaw-freeze-thaw weather and persistent winds—a surface I can often walk on if I dare, without falling through, an icy deck erected over the garden, a giant baked Alaska. It was—and sometimes is—like being cut off from my most elemental self; so painful, the estrangement of those months.

Gardening had been my refuge for many years by then, a hobby cultivated when my widowed mother, just forty-nine, became confused and my only sister needed me to come and help sort things out. The investigation revealed the Alzheimer's and landed me in the home of my childhood again for several years, cutting down the overgrown privet hedges and yews—a self-imposed occupational therapy by day, before evenings spent editing copy at the *New York Times.* All the while I oversaw her increasing needs and the chaos of family finances that results whenever doctors and lawyers and social workers and caregivers converge on such a crisis.

Even then, when I had no botanical Latin or any confidence in what I was doing, gardening had been my first moving meditation, my yoga. Later, when my mother could stay home no more and the house was no longer ours, the same feeling overtook me upstate: When I was weeding, I was really weeding, those early years at the little house; I was in it as if it were the motions of a *vinyasa*—deepening my connection to the place, to this impossible piece of lopsided land.

I admit it: I garden because I cannot help myself.

It is no wonder so much of gardening is done on one's knees; this practice of horticulture is a wildly humbling way to pass one's days on Earth. Even the root of the word *humility* comes from the soil: from the Latin *humus*, for earth or ground, and a good soil is rich in the partially decayed plant and animal material called humus. Humbled or no, *gardener* was the label imprinted on me when the souls were handed out, and so be it. Gardener. The challenge: to make that cohabit inside me with "corporate publishing executive," the persona I'd taken on from my newspaper-executive father, I suppose, but not been born with.

To be a gardener is to come face-to-face with powerlessness (not something written anywhere in the corporate mission statements of Martha or my two previous employers), and to cultivate patience as actively as you do botanical things. In spite of following all the directions gleaned from Grandma and from garden books, despite considerable years of hands-on experiments and personal access to some of the most knowledgeable masters of the breed, I know only one thing for certain about gardening now, thirty years in:

Things will die.

Oh, and usually they will do so just when they're really starting to look good, after heroic measures of love and many dollars spent; after you have grown very attached. Minimizing your losses isn't part of the picture.

The heavens will fail to provide manna in the form of rain, and send violent, leaf-shredding hail instead; the neighbor's dog will piss on the treasure you grew from a cutting, and it will perish. "Where's my vining *Aconitum*?" you wonder out loud, feeling vaguely ill. The mow-and-blow guys (if you can find anyone who will mow a tricky place like this—I cannot) will say they *thought it was a weed, lady*, and therefore whacked it (and very thoroughly at that: well done). *You're fired.*

The garden is where there's no pretending that living things don't die.

Whatever you don't kill makes you stronger, though, and hungrier for more plants and then some more, and so this imprint deepens: Curiosity becomes interest, interest becomes hobby, hobby becomes passion, passion becomes life's work, and even spiritual pursuit—the stuff of the heart.

Gardening was my first moving-meditation practice, long before I knew that meditation could take place while moving (like the Buddhist walking meditation), long before I knew of formal meditation at all.

When I was raking, I raked—in the moment of raking awareness, neither thinking in shoulda, coulda, woulda monkey mind, nor wandering into daydreams, past or future. Being truly at attention and one with the task: That sense of perfect union was what I had not found anywhere else, and certainly not at work (or at least not since the early years, before I had become "successful").

The Zen master speaks of chopping wood, carrying water. The gardener will know what it is to really be in the moment when she does her most rote, insistent chores. Knowing that, I garden this way: I practice a blend of horticultural how-to and woo-woo, and the view both outside and inward are far better for the fact. I practiced increasing horticultural excess, yes, those back and forth weekender years, but I also practiced communion and some moments of peace. In short: My garden saved me.

"Your garden is amazing," people say when they come touring by the hundreds on garden open days I've held for charity the last thirteen years. "How did it get this way?"

"This is what happens when you stay in one place for twenty years," I tell them, "and just keep digging more holes." (It also helps if you are mightily trying to escape something, I suppose, and work at that escape as if you are taking a flat bar to clapboards and shingles or Sheetrock to pry them off; if you have ever done demolition, or staged war on an acre of sharp, invasive brambles—real or imagined—that want to choke you and everything around you, then you will know the energy I am speaking of.)

No, you don't end up in China as Mommy said all those years ago would happen if you dug and dug and dug from this side of the Earth. You end up right here, right now—and speaking not Chinese at all, but passable botanical Latin, punctuated with some key Buddhist phrases for good measure, or maybe my own made-up outdoor language in which some Hindi and a lot of *Hello, baby, Mommy loves you*, all fuse into a delightful gibberish—or at least it delights me, and the creatures—the frogs and birds and plants and cat—do not in any obvious manner object.

My depth of connection to gardening, my elemental drive to be one with it, to meld with other living things who do not yell or put forth unrealistic expectations, had probably plotted my course to Copake Falls, New York, and also the one to yoga; had made them my magnetic north. That word—*yoga*—meaning a yoking or union is what I surely felt outdoors, and what I came to feel on the mat when in desperation I sought a wintertime refuge from the dominant element of my life, from work; from all that static of the frequency I mostly lived on.

I didn't buy cute outfits for my yoga; I didn't ever do it in a place like a health club that felt anything less than sacred. I sought peace and clarity, and so, as with the gardening, I took it seriously, and it was from the start a religious thing, a time of meditation and of healing. Both were on the order of devotional for me, from the first encounter between us.

But then even this one pure practice, which started out so simply, eventually took the hit from my increasing mania, my overload, my madness at being trapped and stifled and under one too many layers of sheathing myself, at being not-Margaret (and also, of course, not-Martha, but rather in the backup band), at doing and not being. And so instead of one hundred dollars a month for an unlimited class card at the very crunchy yoga studio I had settled into, where the best part was the chanting and where I was often brought to tears from the first asana or breath or Sanskrit sound, I was soon turning up the volume, plotting my course to the promise of yoga deluxe. I was so numb.

In winter, done in by the obsession of the workweek and temporarily abandoned by my suddenly frigid lover the garden, I eventually made a practice of dropping a lot of money at the premium spas around the United States. Like I said, the longest journey begins with a single check. (But caveat emptor: It doesn't stop at one.)

"If there's a retail path to enlightenment, Maggie, I think you're a shoo-in," my friend and fellow seeker Dave had said more than once those years, when I was busy retreating and re-retreating, coming home with stacks of books each time that teetered here in the once-weekend house on each end table and beside each chair, threatening to crash to the floor: *Attention, attention!* They were my towers of wisdom stuffed with shreds of paper to mark the best bits, their endpapers penciled with my frantic handwriting, my bulleted lists, all the secrets I didn't want to forget, *oh no please let me remember the secrets, please.* Nearby, there were towers of song, too: the mounting stacks of CDs as yet not grouped, alphabetized, filed.

I don't like thinking of myself as shopping for serenity; so much shame derives from recalling how it took more and more and more to get through to me as the months wore on, more and more and more to quiet me down, *just one more sip* and then another (you name which nectar), *oh please just one.*

THE YOGA AND MEDITATION GETAWAYS had started innocently enough at popular retreat centers such as Kripalu and Omega, American meccas for those who are searching for connection to the spirit, places where there were no aquacise classes or indoor tennis courts. And they'd even taken me to the World Trade Center, speaking of places that would attain hallowed status. Whatever the price tag, and no matter how far off course I occasionally veered, there was magic in each of my adventures, and this was no exception.

I had broken from my country-weekend-or-bust tradition and stayed in the city June 29 to July 1, 2001, to attend *Tricycle* magazine's tenth anniversary conference, "Buddhism: Does It Make a Difference?" with top thinkers from around the world. In line at registration that first morning at the Marriott that stood between the Twin Towers, I saw him, his blond hair now longer and in a ponytail, but definitely him:

My ex-psychiatrist, a longtime personal guide but from an entirely different lineage of truth-tellers, was just ahead of me in line. How strange to see him after having parted years before, having "finished" our work; how awkward to see him in his real life, a life I knew nothing of in the best and strictest psychiatric tradition. We said hello, and then set off on our individual curriculums within the giant conference, occasionally finding ourselves in the same room again. It felt deeply odd to be sharing the intimacy and connectedness of the meditation sessions with this person, a different kind of silence than the one I had so often enforced with him in years past in my stubbornness against really looking inside, when we sat together one-on-one, with the meter running.

Circle and circle as I may have, here we are again, face-to-face. Yes, it's me: the grievous angel, as Gram Parsons dubbed it, still a tad wretched but still at it, twenty thousand side roads later. *Hello, Dr. Goudard; how are you?*

To this minute I think that Eric V. Goudard, MD, was in that line that day at that hotel between those towers just for me, so that I would know the number to dial when the events right there unfolded two and a half months hence. He had been sent maybe fifteen years before to my hospital room as the psychiatric resident on duty after residents and pulmonologists who'd treated me all night in the ER thought I seemed "stressed out." Send the little lady a shrink; *Go find that young Dr. Goudard, why don't you? Let him deal with this gasping loon. Stat.*

It was during the Caring for Mommy Years. I had a punctured lung, my second time around on that very uncommon score, once again resulting from chronic coughing related to my asthma. Not being able to breathe—and listening to the sound of your right lung emptying some of its contents into your body, a high-pitched leak in a balloon hissing, hissing, the air looking for somewhere to escape to—can in fact make a girl a little nervous and distraught. Yes, it was stressful. So is puffing up like the Michelin man or an oversize roll of bubble wrap as the air makes a subcutaneous pit stop on its way out: right arm and neck and face like an overblown rag doll. Yes, Dr. Goudard and I had been through some violent moments, right from the start.

The phones in New York were so difficult just after 9 / 11, and psychiatrists like him in such demand, that we did not hear each other's voices again until the evening of September 25, when Dr. Goudard reached me back on my cell phone as I was standing in another line of Buddhists: this one to hear the Vietnamese monk and peace activist Thich Nhat Hanh deliver a talk called "Embracing Anger" at Riverside Church on Manhattan's Upper West Side, his gift of comfort to a stricken city.

"I am having a hard time," I said, surely a sentence he had heard one thousand or maybe ten thousand times the previous two weeks. "Can I come see you?"

Fast forward through several years including some resumed sessions—the doctor's mantra or measure of reality always the same, no matter what topic we are discussing: *Is it good enough, Margaret?*—and I am walking into a class one late fall afternoon in Arizona, at the Miraval resort.

I had fled to this place after a planned trip to Asia with a not-good-enough man I loved then had fallen apart last moment, the casualty of fear on both sides (his of togetherness; mine of travel, which I am very, very bad at, and of course of togetherness, too). I'd quickly scanned the high-end destination headlines for a lead, determined to show the man (who traveled for a living, or I would say escaped regularly, a convenient series of hall passes granted by his job) that I was not a baby, that I could go on an adventure, could get on a plane. First class to Tucson through O'Hare, then ushered from the airport to the spa, wasn't exactly adventure travel in the Third World, but the light in the American desert has always calmed me, and made me cry. Some of both was called for, and off I went, alone.

I was meant to be in Nepal, finally meeting the residents of a remote mountaintop village of three thousand people whom the traveling man and I had loosely adopted the previous couple of years, after he discovered their world on one of his own magical mystery tours. But (big surprise) I am in yet another fancy American spa lobby, at the registration desk, my same black Tumi duffel beside me, stuffed with my standard uniform of black tank tops, yoga pants, and thick cotton socks, and several annotated books checked out from the vast wisdom collection housed in the living room back home.

Next step (after the credit card imprint, after some higher power across a digital network approved the transaction): The program adviser at Miraval asked me what the intention of my vacation was, the way they always do at these places, the way I'd been asked so many times before. *What is your intention?* I have no memory of what I said, but she urgently sent me scurrying with some marked-up handouts about a man named Jonathan, whose classes, she said, I must not fail to attend. One was starting shortly. *Hurry.*

He had a ponytail, I remember, and old-fashioned wire-rimmed spectacles, and a string of beads lay tight against his throat. Perhaps fifteen or twenty years my junior, Jonathan Ellerby, PhD, has the clearest eyes I've ever seen, expectant eyes full of light. Was it the glint off the spectacles or some inner glow? At this juncture, and coming from the place where I found myself internally, it really did not matter; a familiar pony-tail, and light from any direction shining on me would do just fine. After all, I had learned the secret of fire from Herb, hadn't I?—a high school science teacher I'd mistaken for a farmer—so by comparison, this was tame, and if it sucked, well, I had a massage booked later on.

We sat on the floor of the conference room in a circle, and Jonathan passed around the handouts he'd meticulously prepared:

> *She who sees deeply into one thing, sees all.*
> *She who looks long into all things, sees nothing.*
>
> —ANCIENT VEDIC TEACHING, C. 4000 BCE

On the next page, this:

> *If you want to be given everything,*
> *Give everything up . . .*
> *Because the Master has no goals in mind,*
> *Everything she does succeeds.*
>
> —LAO TZU, C. 600 BCE

You talkin' to me? I thought when I glanced at them while people got settled, just as when I'd found the various bits I had marked up and penciled into the endpapers of my stacks of books back home. And then, on the next two pages, were shiny young Jonathan's own teachings, "The 12 Paradoxes of the Sacred Path":

1. Do your inner work to address your outer challenges.
2. Be willing to give all, to get all.

51

3. All the answers you seek are within you now, and you'll need a path, a guide and time.

4. Be focused, discerning, and determined, and surrender to mystery in each moment.

5. That which takes from us, gives to us: Sickness is healer, loss is a teacher.

6. Master suffering and self-discipline to understand joy and freedom.

7. You must come to terms with death, to embrace life.

8. Your feelings are as important as they are misleading.

9. Be compassionately indifferent.

10. Learn the power of solitude and the importance of community.

11. That which is invisible is real and lasting, the visible is a fleeting lie: Spirit is the driving force behind matter.

12. Live your authentic, true self, and know that it too is an illusion.

Some curriculum; I should perhaps extend my stay to twenty years, or twenty lifetimes. But I love lists (*checking it twice!*), and I already love Jonathan and the program adviser who sent me to Jonathan and the wandering boyfriend and everyone on the planet and possibly other planets, too. *Be grateful to everyone* never seemed so easy as in this moment, even at the exorbitant day rate.

And so I spend a private session hour on each of the next days walking in the desert with Jonathan and picking up stones as he instructs, talking about what each one meant to me, about whom each stone represented, placing it somewhere in relation to the stones already gathered in the hopes of telling him a story (at his prompting) about what was going on with these stones I'd chosen among all the possible stones out there; a story about me, a story about *what is your intention?* A stone for each parent, one for my sister, one for the flyaway man, one for me.

I know: *insane* (and I also get a really wicked sunburn in the process—not quite the fully transformative reptilian skin-shedding I badly need but a symbolic step in the right direction, an itchy reminder; so noted). While Jonathan and I are out here in the desert anthropomorphizing rocks, I realize that Dr. Goudard, who is actually a child psychiatrist by specialty, is probably back in New York playacting with his chronologically younger patients this way, but using wooden blocks or plastic figures instead.

I have always liked stones, and guides with ponytails, and having my shoulders peel makes me feel like a child again who stayed too long at the pool, reading one yellow-spined Nancy Drew Mystery Stories volume after another; and instead of a proper lunch eating golden French fries with so much salt and with ketchup that didn't come in a packet.

When I am not in a class with Jonathan or a private session playing with stones with Jonathan I am doing yoga or just staring at the sky. Or I am seeing snakes.

"Well, what you're describing is a king snake," the Miraval nature guide says when I go to his office in the main building to ask him what it is I have almost just stepped on on my way to the yoga hut. "But they aren't really around this time of year—you just don't see them now."

Right.

By the time my little trip is done, the back sides of all Jonathan's classroom handouts are filled with his not-quite-childlike handwriting: big block-capital-printed letters, the summary notes he methodically sends you away with each day, usually in the form of more lists. That's how Jonathan works: He writes notes to you to take home. And if you're smart, you save them.

The first list he gave me, his wrap-up of our initial chat that hadn't been billed to be exactly about this at all, or at least not as so stated: "BECAUSE OF FEAR—WHAT I WON'T DO."

Yes, of course, all the usual suspects were on it: snakes and air travel, fear of getting very sick with asthma when there was no way to get help, claustrophobia, *being away from home*. The punch line: If I stay afraid of all this stuff I will stay in my routine, my comfort zone—which at this moment in life is (*shit; now here's a wrinkle*) none too comfortable.

The other list was about a man, as my other lists always were, the man who was in Nepal without me, and "WHAT HE SYM-BOLIZES," as Jonathan's printing frames it.

My last ponytailed guide hadn't written things down, at least not for takeaway. But the Big Cheese, as I prefer to call Dr. Goudard after all the years we have endured, could have writ-ten those lists of Jonathan's without talking to me ever again, for they were the same old lists I'd dragged around forever, even longer than the Cheese has known me. His version would have been penned in beautiful, old-fashioned cursive letters that are almost feminine; I have not known another man with handwrit-ing such as the Cheese's. But whether set down in block capitals or near-calligraphy, it would be my same old list. Every one of us has one.

If I let myself become embarrassed at all that I have spent to find my way closer to home, and how many guides I have required to even set the process in motion, I'd never speak of any of it again. I'd needed to tell my story again and again only so that I could finally hear it, of course, and really bear witness to myself. I had been for so many years stuck in the predicament of chronic, repetitive tale-telling, with the best to hope for that each successive audience responded by offering at least one small clue in return, in repayment for my latest dramatic reading—and often for my cash.

No, I could not start the fire under myself any more than I could have burned that giant heap of piled-up debris all those years ago at the edge of the property here. My old notebooks scream with the voice of someone who wants out, but just doesn't see the door. We all need the occasional emotional rescue, and I am grateful, if also a bit ashamed, to have required the equivalent of a newspaper-stuffed steel-belted radial to flip my own ignition, too.

MOMENTS OF INCREASINGLY HORRIFIC, SHAMING self-awareness—particularly one that occurred while taking a week off to garden here with my friend Charles—told me how far from all right I had become, how close to all wrong. That loudest of wake-up calls was (embarrassing to acknowledge) over a little-known plant called *Hylomecon japonicum*, an ephemeral Asian woodlander that sends up poppylike gold flowers in early spring, then tucks itself back underneath the ground to lay dormant until its name is called again a year hence, asking nothing in the meantime except that you do not forget its hidden presence and take a shovel to it in unconscious haste.

I had at the time grown this perennial for maybe ten years, perhaps longer—this plant that nobody, even most experts, had ever heard of or grown. It wasn't on the market until a couple of years ago, and then only in one mail-order place and for a considerable bounty. I got my one precious little *Hylomecon* at a sale at the New England Wild Flower Society in Framingham, Massachusetts, one spring when they were selling not just American natives but also some of their Asian counterparts or close cousins, of which there are so many such examples owing to the likes of plate tectonics and a land bridge that spanned the Bering Strait not so many thousands of years ago—owing to such sea changes of a more literal nature than mine. What was breaking apart in the story of this plant of mine, though, was me: I had become brittle, and crusty, prime material for a big shift.

I was working in the garden one early spring week a decade ago with Charles and his partner, Glenn—wildly talented friends from Seattle who came a number of times to help me sort the place out when I was trying to transition it from "a good start" to something better. I was in the backyard, hoicking garlic mustard and other unwanted somethings out of the ground to clear a new bed, and then as I passed the front of the house to empty my wheelbarrow in the compost heap beyond, I saw him: Charles, standing by the porch, cutting something into little bits. There was a hole in the moist, cool earth where *my precious plant* had been; no forensics were required to unravel that he had—without asking—dug up *my plant* and simply begun slicing and dicing.

I began to shout, and not because there was a great distance between us that required the volume. I began to shout at Charles, to scream threateningly at this very tall, startled man whom I adore and respect beyond measure—and then I burst into tears that would not stop.

Those were the days when any piece of my puzzle put even momentarily out of place could do it to me: Out of control sent me out of my mind. I could not imagine living without my *Hylomecon* growing *right over there* where I had put it (*check*) or with the thought of its certain death from dismemberment.

Each year now in late April onward, my eyes are rubbed in a reminder of that day when my precious plant was divided and conquered and then liberated, too: Now the mother of thousands, its progeny positively carpet my place. Set free by Charles from the congested spot I'd let it languish and suffer in, diced up to discard any tired, woody bits and favor the tender green parts instead, each piece then replanted with some room to spread its roots and flourish—all of it was a little scary at first, being yanked up out of the earth, but all for the best. Thank you, Charles; uprooting and even breaking apart are sometimes not so bad after all, and just what's called for.

I HAD MEANT TO LEAVE MY JOB FOR SO LONG I had become the Girl Who Cried Martha, but these patient men (yes, I am aware that most of those I listen to have been men—for better or for worse, for richer or for poorer) all kept listening, anyway. Perhaps the only reason I ever finally made the break: I eventually embarrassed myself so thoroughly I had nowhere left to go but forward, having run out of places to comfortably theorize about the *possibility* of doing so any longer.

Even I was sick of me. Thank goodness for those momentary flashes—those out-of-body split seconds when we step away from the part that's speaking and hear the semi-disembodied voice reciting whatever "it" is yet again. Enough tripe; *oh, shut up and do something.*

I'd meant to leave a couple of years after Martha Stewart

Living Omnimedia's initial public stock offering and whatever fantasy pot of gold would come to me—remember the days of IPOs? How ludicrous it all seems now. But the inducements aimed at retention increased each round and I just kept saying, *Just the one more year, then I can do it; then I will have enough*. In there also came 2001 with its unimagined feelings of instability and its economic downturns, and so I mentally re-upped, steeled myself for yet another tour of duty. But each resolve was trickier, bordering on insidious.

I retargeted my departure for age fifty, in 2004, reworking my spreadsheets and rechecking that list called "Tolerances" that had been pinned to my city kitchen's wall for years, the edges of the notepaper it was written on now curling from age. Tolerances, as in: How much can you tolerate of what for how long? But then Martha had her tenacious legal troubles, and in their wake the company its own kind, and I stayed on, hunkered down with my surrogate family more hours than ever, working more and then some more, a time punctuated by surreal goings-on like Securities and Exchange Commission depositions and court-room drama and eventually flights to West Virginia, to see my longtime boss and friend when she was denied her liberty, the last one on Valentine's Day with a chocolate in my pocket that would be a violation of the law if I gave it to her. And the band of my split life played on (had someone hired more players for the violin section without telling me?).

I was fifty-one by the time I found myself in Arizona, reading Jonathan's handouts and crying at the pink light of each day's start and finish, and not yet free of either my fears or my job— still shuttling back and forth and back again between the two worlds that were my dissonant aspects, still making lists of what it would take, as if some precise calculation or magic number was the key. As if I could prove the equation mathematically; as if it were a mathematic equation at all. If not for substantial upheaval at the very top of the corporate structure when Martha came home from prison—on the board and in the executive office—and all the intricate changes that trickled down in the aftermath of those moves, I do not think I would have ever loosened my grip on my life.

But I was blessed by the disruptions—*be grateful to everyone*, even the new bosses you don't want to work for, whose hiring made redundant the beloved manager I'd partnered with and grown accustomed to for years. Somehow, thankfully, deep inside my increasingly tiny, withered self, I realized that adapting to this latest incarnation of the company's administration would only dig me in for several more years, as each previous crisis had. I would not flourish, and the chance for that was overdue. This was my moment, and I dragged myself to the finish line of my corporate career.

And so in December 2007, after discussing it for nearly eight months with the new leadership and hashing out a staged separation from five days to two to none at all by midyear 2008, my car and I began parking ourselves in reverse—in our upstate driveway more nights than in the downstate one—and then eventually stopped hurtling back and forth so much altogether.

We will both live longer as a result, the Saab and I.

I've decided to go live in the woods (it's for the best).

Chapter 3

And Away We Go
(At Last)

IT IS QUIET HERE IN A WAY THAT'S HARD TO DESCRIBE, a way that makes you notice when there is noise, the same-but-different way that you are instantly alerted when (if) there is a silence in the nonstop auditory havoc that is the urban environment.

It is quiet here—particularly in November through March, when hikers and bicyclists disappear, when weekenders don't visit their part-time homes so often, when everybody stays in and stokes the stove.

"Are you certain that you want to start your retirement in the winter?" the kind but persistent Dr. Goudard had been asking through the year previous to my departure, while the negotiations were under way. "Is that wise?" (Just another version of his *Is it good enough?*, that perennial question against which all decisions have been weighed in the on-and-off twenty-plus years of our conversation.)

I moved to the woods to get away from noise: from all the other voices but my own, to hunker down and listen, really listen, but even in this place, in the dead of winter, even when I lie at night in my big bed that (because of the way the house is situated on a steep incline) is in the treetops, turning bedroom into a refuge like a tree house, there are voices sounding insistently—and not just Dr. Goudard's, with whom I agreed to continue phone sessions every other Tuesday evening, a kind of compromise that earned me my conditional release from urban confinement.

Attention, attention! says the spiritual teacher, yes, but so do the other living creatures whose space, after all, I have now invaded. The house lets me hear its noises more unashamedly than when we were in our long-distance phase; intimacy, and shacking up with a loved one, are filled with surprising sounds not emitted in the honeymoon stages. And even the unheard sensory dimensions of the place—the light, most notably, the insistent and indescribable light of this area where the Hudson Valley of New York State meets the Berkshire Mountain range of Massachusetts—keep telling me to pay it mind, to focus, to be present. *Watch me; I will show you where to look, and when.*

A pair of bluebirds is already signed on to stay with me through this first winter, it seems, something that's not rare as much as just unusual: to have bluebirds in the coldest months here, when they can easily travel somewhere just slightly more favorable. It hasn't happened before in my twenty-plus years here; we normally say good-bye around October, and renew our relationship in March. Eastern bluebirds (*Sialia sialis*) are partial migrants, and each of their options has its pros and cons: They don't have to go very far or anywhere, really, to survive—they are tough—but they are capable of considerable flight (though not to the tropics). The farther south they head, however, the later they will be back to lay claim to prime nesting spots come spring, so it's a toss-up—an easier winter versus prime real estate for raising a family. All lives involve hard decisions, and compromise.

Perhaps this pair who stayed or stopped here is just plain tired of shuttling back and forth between two homes and decided to skip the trip, as I had lately, or perhaps they want to watch—as my friends and family did—to see what I'm getting into. I am happy for their company, frankly, and for their dry chatter and also the other sound, a liquidy one that is sometimes expressed in bird books as "Tu-a-wee," or transliterated simply into "Truly." (Another reference says it's "Chir-lee," and the Dummies version of that one is, "Cheer, cheer, cheerful, charmer.")

I don't hear words at all, much as the bird-guide authors try to help me do so. *Still a man hears what he wants to hear and disregards the rest*, I keep thinking. Instead of their translation attempts I am happy to simply say that bird sounds are to my ear indescribable in English, but even with that substantial limitation, I am glad for the utterances, especially in this quietest time of the birding year. Conversation is sometimes overrated; cooing and song and even the determined drumming of the woodpecker never grows tiresome. I thank them, every one, as Philippe Petit did in the acknowledgments in *To Reach the Clouds*, when he wrote: "and to that seabird circling over me on the morning of August 7, 1974."

You know where he was then: man on a wire, between two towers, and between dimensions—with his life about to change forever.

Anne Lamott told us to write bird by bird; I am going one step further, I suppose, and living that way, and it pleases me more than the sorting of CDs and mismatched food-storage containers did. Bird by bird; no longer lid by lid. Progress?

I am reading a lot of my many bird books these days, and when I am not reading I am finding myself simply looking out the window, sometimes using my fancy new bigger binoculars, my graduation gift to myself to mark the end of corporate life. Perhaps somewhere in the variable focus of my 10x42 power Stokes DLS's I will catch a glimpse of what I am supposed to do next, I do not know. I have grown aware suddenly that I gave myself not just the big, rubber-coated glasses but also the wi-fi radio. Was I looking for visual, investigative cues and also audio signals that might prove directional? Looking at my new toys, my most-used gear besides the computer on these increasingly cold days spent mostly indoors, I laugh at myself for packing such a seemingly symbolic survival kit. But I am ready for whatever comes, or at least I am enjoying that illusion as long as it lasts.

We are not meant to be alone for long, it seems, the bluebirds, the radio, and I. Good thing I bought the glasses.

As the darkest days of the year approach, I am being treated to my first rare-bird sighting of an informal but long birding career, and when it starts nobody believes me—now I am the Girl Who Cried Pine Grosbeak, and the automated system of the Cornell Lab of Ornithology (the place where I file my online bird counts weekly through the fall and winter each year) says at first that it isn't so.

But yes, yes it is. I may be here alone, without anyone to confirm my instinct (a reality that will color more days than just this ornithological occasion as I settle into my new life—as in, *Can I Get a Witness?*), but those are pine grosbeaks at the edge of the woods, checking out my twelve fruit-laden crab apples. I know it, even though I have never seen one before, and when I go outside to take a closer look, I feel even more certain. These characteristically gregarious birds (the books call them "unwary"), two or three males and perhaps a dozen females, don't even stop splashing in the half-frozen frog pond when I come out the back door, not twenty feet away. They're too busy enjoying the hole I keep open in the ice to protect my amphibian friends who slumber in the mucky bottom from suffocating. The deicing setup, a red plastic and metal device not unlike a floating hot plate, apparently reads "birdbath" to these large red-and-taupe-gray-colored birds (the red replaced by yellow olive in the females). Some of them are actually standing on the deicer, a life raft in the little pond, bobbing with the tide that their delirious activity is stirring.

But why are they here? *Learn something new every day*, Martha said, a kind of company and personal mission statement of hers—ours—all those years. And I am. *Pinicola enucleator*—what a powerful name!—has timed its species' first superflight in more than a decade with my own, irrupting along with millions of other so-called winter finches from the boreal forests of Canada, flying great distances to somewhere with a better-stocked pantry than proved to be the case up north this year, where the seed-producing trees and shrubs they normally rely on didn't meet expectations.

An irruption, or in its most extreme a superflight, is not a kind of migration; the latter word indicates a pattern of movement that's repeated year after year. When birds appear far south of their normal wintering grounds in an unpredictable manner, shifting their population density in a big way, you have an irruption or even a superflight; the last time, I quickly learn, had been eleven years earlier, in 1997–1998; before that 1982–1983.

Unable to hibernate like some of my other new animal neighbors here, or enter some self-preserving form of hibernation or diapause like the smallest members of my community (certain of the insects), the birds must move to where the sustenance is, to where they believe they can get what they need to survive. Here, with me. Hallelujah; I am uplifted.

I suppose I have irrupted in reverse, fleeing meager circumstances by moving south to north just in the nick. The twelve crab apple trees that form the primary view from my desk window are now these birds' larder; for my part, I am happy tucked inside, watching them, and I suppose myself, too, every day or two defrosting some colorful Tupperware or Ziploc brick of last season's garden I had packed carefully away in anticipation of my own nutritional needs.

Learn something new every day. Some scientists speculate that the variation in food production that periodically prompts the birds way south of their normal winter home is actually an evolutionary strategy on the part of the plants, which thereby reduce the long-term impact of the otherwise nonstop eating. The plants make less food on purpose—to get the birds out of their hair, like a nursing mother who's just had enough and says *go drink a bottle of formula* instead. I think otherwise: I think that in the winter of my superflight, in 2007–2008, the birds moved south for me. Magical thinking, but these are my maiden magical days.

John Burroughs would have understood: *The observer of bird-life in the open has heaven and earth thrown in.*

And this is how the first days are going, frankly; I am reduced to the rank of observer, having forgone my doing and directing roles. Seeing rare birds gives me purpose, and that is something I am seeking with a passion similar to their interest in all that frozen fruit dangling from those dormant trees of mine.

I am back to shopping for serenity in a big way, as another bout of book buying has taken hold. Apparently my standards have fallen away along with my career and my "future" and any obvious rhythm to my days, and now it's not just verging on self-help but in the thick of it, books from the section that should be labeled Pulp Nonfiction with titles or subtitles that promise "Ten Steps to…" and "Yes, You Can.…" Oh, dear. (About this time I have started to notice that my selections at the wine store are getting cheaper, too. Coincidence, or across-the-board desperation?)

Perhaps I should have just bought another bird book today when I tucked into the local bookseller's (though I don't think there is a one I do not have). But no; ornithology was not the take home, nor was another translation of the Upanishads or volume of mystical thirteenth-century Sufi poetry. Instead on this wintry day I find myself at the kitchen table with a purple-covered volume called *The Passion Test*, its promise an "effortless path to discovering your destiny." Sounds like just what's called for; why am I so ashamed, and wanting to wrap it in one of those plain brown covers fashioned from a paper bag, even though I am here alone and nobody else can see?

PLEASE TURN TO PAGE 43: A lavender-tinted box, meant to represent the index card I am supposed to use for the exercise, is labeled "MY PASSION TEST." A space for the date is next, and then the prompt "When my life is ideal I am…" and five blank lines after that. Beneath the fifth empty space I'm meant to fill in, there is a kicker, a school cheer:

"This or something better!" (Shades of Dr. Goudard's *Is it good enough?*)

Okay, this is not exactly a pearl of passion wisdom. Pearls or hogwash, I never turn past page 43. But in the earlier going, this passionately purple book did get me to engage: The first part of the Passion Test is simply (or not so simply) to list ten things that are most important: what I will "be, do or have when [my] life is ideal."

Oh, shit.

On February 19, 2008, in no particular order, I set down in pencil (tentative, was I?) into a new orange-covered note-book my desires, my Passion Test V1.0. Using the same operating principle as my index-card-and-pushpin-covered corkboard upstairs, the book stressed not to edit yourself this first time out; just get it all down. And so I did. *When my life is ideal I am…*

1. Being surrounded by plants, gardening madly.
2. Watching birds.
3. Listening to music; sharing it.
4. Having sex…a lot.
5. Cooking for others.
6. Changing 3,000 lives (and teaching those 3,000 to each change 3,000 lives).
7. Reading with eagerness and excitement.
8. Writing with abandon and success.
9. Traveling fearlessly.
10. Living without fear of asthma.

How am I doing? Always the editor and ever the rule breaker, I cannot help but look at my list with a critical eye and a pen in hand. And so:

1. Okay, there are lots of plants out there, but the ground is frozen.
2. Great job; exceptional.
3. Thank you, wi-fi radio and those reorganized CDs.
4. and also,
5. both require human company. Hmmmm...
6. The work in Nepal is going nicely, second school rebuilt; attendance up.
7. Yes, but only if you give credit for bird books and pop self-help titles.
8. Neither.
9. Increasingly, I don't even leave the property.
10. I wonder if this one will ever be far from front of mind?

And then I ponder the list, and winnow it to the home runs, the real sweet spots, as I am told to do by my newest $23.95 guide. My list in its most essential form:

1. Gardening offline and online.
2. Changing 3,000 lives.
3. Having lots of great sex.
4. Writing a bestseller.
5. Living without asthma.

Maybe I need another kind of help.

Pragmatism in Perpetual Motion

THERE ARE CHALLENGES TO LIVING ALONE, none of which, for me—at least not these days—involves loneliness or want of company. Instead, my issues with living life alone center on danger and on dignity, a pair of words that fight each other for the upper hand in judgments that I make each day in my new life. It is a little like being a baby songbird—they are altricial, meaning requiring nourishment and basically helpless—except you don't outgrow it.

I reach the point of mental tension regularly: Something happens and I need help, and I'm just not sure which is worse: the need for help, or the attendant humiliation of what it is I need being revealed to another. Usually I just sit here bleeding alone, or drenched in my frustration if I have caused myself no bodily harm, hoping it will stop in time.

Sometimes, especially on days when I am frazzled from some string of life's irritations or haven't slept enough, I lose the ability to tell what's normal—whether it's time to call out or just to sit here, looking out the window awhile longer for the signal I know will come.

I hope it is soon. *What time is it, anyway?*

I do not wear a watch, and haven't in decades. For thirty-two years, I counted on the day to work like this form of clockwork:

- Awaken. Drink very strong black tea with extra milk and one sugar, one to two cups, as had my grandfather before me (though I skipped the belt of whiskey he put in his).

- Shower, wash hair, dry hair, apply makeup, dress, check to see if you have your earrings in.
- Curse while finding keys, get in car / on subway / on bus (depending on what year it was and where I lived) and go to work.
- Stay there for a long time, and then some. Do whatever is on the calendar, which somebody else has arranged in your behalf, just as if this is not your life.
- Come home. Eat standing in front of the refrigerator (low-fat cheese, though I am 5 feet 6 inches tall and weighed 106, and the plainest crackers) or the microwave (typically one Amy's Organic frozen dinner per night).
- Sleep.
- Repeat.

I know: "Check to see you have your earrings in" is the part of that list that doesn't fit, exactly, the one that would be the answer if this were a "Which item doesn't go with all the others?" question on a standardized intelligence test. I have always found it very disturbing to go out without my earrings, at once alarmed and even panicky when some subconscious message of *you forgot, you forgot* would send my hand up to a lobe, over and again, disbelieving but also confirming what the intact-if-a-bit-unplugged mind already knew.

There was no chance I would have left the house without makeup; since my midteens, I've worn it daily, and I would sooner go out naked into the street than without foundation, mascara, lipstick—the works. But those earrings got away from me sometimes, and on the mornings I forgot them (which happened perhaps three or four times each year despite the fact that it was on the checklist), I'd need to add another step to the list:

- Go downstairs to Fifth Avenue to buy a cheap pair at the jeweler's, a simple little pair of silver hoops for perhaps twelve dollars. *No bag, thanks; I'll wear them. Ah! That's better.*

This is the kind of thing that happens when your life is out of control, some compulsive disorder earring thing, I suppose, though at the time I thought it was just some vestige of my upbringing, an echo of my grandma's admonitions about being ladylike, and Emily Post-ish. *Elbows off the table, girls.* Or: *Mind that your slip's not showing.* Essentially slipless in modern days, my sense of equilibrium-cum-OCD had turned to those damn earrings, vested in magical powers by me, who was unable to manage without them in the corporate world, Samson without his locks.

It is Month 3 of my freedom and I still drink the tea as Step 1, grateful for that small consistency. The rest? Well, as Grandma also used to say with regularity and as just keeps seeming like the phrase of the day: *To hell in a handbasket.*

At this point I am looking for any lead on how to catch the beat of things, get the rhythm. I was grateful at first that Garbage Night (no, not a book club or dinner date but Garbage Night, in capital letters) provided another anchor to the week; perhaps not the perfect matched bookend to all those first-thing-each-day cups of tea, but something. Garbage Night, on Sundays for the Monday morning pickup, was something that I counted on. Eastern Rural Time (or is it Eastern Unemployment Time?) is a slippery thing, though. You never know when the carting company will change Garbage Night, and then you're down to one reliable moment each day: that cup of tea.

On a list in my orange notebook, observations from December 8, 2008:

- Saving so much time not "getting ready" for work (makeup, clothes, etc.).
- Often shower at night now, for first time in my life.
- Carrying a handbag is incongruous with way I now dress—need knapsack?
- Hoodies and socks: in pursuit of really good ones.

Note to self re: making notes to self: Uh-oh. And soon the saying-it-out-loud portion of the program begins; writing it in the notebook isn't getting me anywhere, so I have started speaking it, a cappella status reports, though without much tangible status to report. Uh-oh, to the tenth power.

One day the calls for help or more specifically about the utter frustration of helplessness are said aloud, too, tangled in a mess with self-chastising words sparked by those can't-do feelings: *Margaret, you asshole.*

Even inanimate objects are targets. And then it happens: You finally let it bubble up to consciousness that you hate the chair in the dining room where you sit to work each morning, the chair beside the window with the very best light in the house, nearly due west, and opposite a window that is nearly due east, so this particular chair gets it coming and going.

Every window in the little house has its equal and opposite partner—like Isaac Newton's third law. Depending on the time of day, the action of one seems to cause an equal and opposite reaction in the other as light passes across the house at key hours that vary according to the time of year. If you stand looking out one and turn around, either twenty feet (the width of the house) or thirty feet away (its length), you get the axial view.

The hell with nice light, at this moment, though, because you want to move the chair, whose cushion slips from its spot on the chair frame so that before long each day your ass is in an abyss (would that it were only your ass, and not your whole life); your back is bowed against its normal curve and aching in the way backs can after a long, unpleasant ride in a rental car, whose seat you simply cannot adjust to suit because you are holding a map, looking for your glasses, and oh, yes, the car is already in gear and moving forward. The chair is inhospitable, but allowing this to rise up and be heard (often even said aloud) in a place where no one else can hear seems, well, silly, though truthfully I am hearing my voice speaking out loud more often than it did mere months ago, sometimes startling me (probably another bad sign).

This is a stupid fucking chair, I said to the dining room one Tuesday morning, one of those March days when winter was giving spring another go. *This is a stupid fucking chair.* The chair I am disparaging in full voice is positioned as the best seat in the place, but it is not the best seat.

A tree died to make the window that the stupid fucking chair sits beside into the best window in the house. I don't mean the tree that the boards were hewn from in the 1880s to actually make the window frame and trim and sill inside and out, but a tree not so long ago, just as I was readying myself to move here. A tree that stood fifteen feet from this window for most of a century finally let go as if to make this my sunny spot in wintertime, to help make me at home. (More magical thinking, I know, but it worked for Einstein; *live as if everything is a miracle.* Like Newton's, his thinking is welcome here, unless anybody else has got any answers?)

I did so love that tree, a long-needled pine of a very unusual shape, like a two-and-a-half-story bonsai. It sacrificed itself for me, so that I could sit in the light all day, while I tried to find my rhythm, my direction; while I learned again to tell time and direction and figuratively to tie my shoes (or at least put some on and actually go somewhere).

I want to move this chair in the worst way, but there are obstacles: It is too heavy to lift, and too big if left upright for the doorway it must wedge through, and anyway, its feet will scratch the painted floor if I push instead of lift. But most of all this: *I could hurt myself.*

How I hate those four words, but how familiar they have quickly become. It's the phrase I hear each time I take a knife from the wooden block on the counter; each time I maneuver the steep path from door to car and back again on the season's endless ice; each time I pry a partly opened can lid out from on top of the desired pinto beans inside; each time the rubber mat (yes, I must use one here; shades of Grandma and Rubbermaid) in the giant claw-foot bathtub that is also my shower slips an inch before grabbing tight to the worn porcelain beneath. *I could hurt myself.*

Proud of my independence, I am also limited by it, and so there must be rules: *No climbing ladders when you are alone,* even though some outdoor light has blown, or the window fan stashed in the attic must be had at once to handle a sudden bout of early heat, or a branch is torn in the magnolia and wants removing before it rips a long strip of bark from the trunk, dangling precariously as it is. *No mowing on the tractor on alone days*, nor any other tractor duty then. When would someone find me if I tipped on this impossible piece of Tilt-A-Whirl land? Who would find me? *I've fallen and I can't get up.*

And so the master rule of rules: *Keep a separate list of to-dos involving a chaperone*, and wait for Susan, my alter ego in the garden and all-purpose partner in minor home repairs. Or I look for Herb, if he is passing by in the purple truck he drives these days, the one he got a steal on, I would wager, owing to its off-color. I wave him down and ask for a hand.

But frankly, it's embarrassing, this waiting to snare someone passing by, this *While you're here could you just help me with a thing or two?* To my ear, *I need you to help so I can change a lightbulb* is so devoid of pioneer spirit, a bad joke in the vein of those "How many (fill in the blanks) does it take to change a lightbulb?" but just not funny, and so transparently lacking any element whatsoever of *she's got what it takes* that I almost do not recognize the voice who is speaking these requests.

But that is my voice, and *I could hurt myself.* On Susan's next workday, we move the chair and change the outdoor lightbulb in the gable end of Jack's cabin. The tasks take six minutes and then four more, but I have waited a week leading up to the solutions. I grow tame here in the woods.

I WANT TO BE ALONE.

I am still on the spin cycle, and I just want to be alone. I have read books, and watched birds, and upped my Netflix to the six-at-a-time plan, consuming every episode of every season of all the things I *never had time* to watch: *Weeds* and *The Wire* and *Wire in the Blood* and *Six Feet Under* and *Big Love* and *Cracker* and *Mad Men* and *MI-5* and *Huff* and more, every last disc of each, rat-a-tat-tat, sometimes indulging in five- or even six-disc stretches in whole days under the duvet in my big bed, accompanied by my extremely serious heating pad of therapeutic caliber, the Princess and the Red-Hot Pea.

I have caught every episode of Season 1 of Gabriel Byrne's premiere installment of *In Treatment* on HBO; I have slept well (smack in the middle of my king-size bed, because when you live alone there are no sides; even land grabs like sleeping decisions are delightfully unanimous in a dictatorship). I have gone for walks and made myself proper suppers of roasted brussels sprouts and root vegetables and homemade pizza—filling the house with the scent of yeast dough rising in a bowl covered with a fresh dish towel on the steel countertop—and all manner of pasta dishes with my own defrosted garden sauce, and I am still on the spin cycle.

Like a kid in the car with Mommy and Daddy, saying, *"Are we there yet?"* I am impatient for it to start feeling like vacation, or better yet for some epiphanic state to overcome me—for something besides spinning to become the blue plate special here, the table d'hôte.

Have you tried to force a washer, its well-named agitator and spin basket still whirling madly, to *stop right now*? Even turning off the power, even unplugging, does not do it; there is so much residual torque built up that it insists on taking its own time, and meantime taking you for the ride. One would risk the literal limb to intervene. *Steamroller.* A person could get crushed around here.

Having been in perpetual motion for so many years, it hurts to sit still unless there are ample DVDs, and enough wine. It hurts. Heat-seeking missiles like a target, a to-do list, a mission plan. *Get me Mission Control: When do we launch this puppy?*

I just want to be alone, but someone (and from the sounds of it, their expanding family along with them) is living in the bedroom wall, scratching at night as if perhaps I ought to pay closer attention, as if maybe they have some message I need to hear. *Everybody's trying to be my baby.*

I grow tamer, scaling no heights when unchaperoned and taking extra care around sharp objects, and my semiwild cat grows tamer, too, wanting to come indoors and spend the days with me as he gradually sees that I do not leave so much anymore (and more to the point: between the two of us, I have the better heating system).

There is a lot of trust in even his suggested few hours of daily indoor time these last cold months because I do not have a cat door on my house. He can come and go at will from his own cabin, which has one; at my place, just twenty feet away across the apron of fieldstones that form a sort of landing pad for both our places, who stays and goes and when they do so is up to me. The Big House cannot have a cat door or Margaret would be living with raccoons and possums and skunks and whomever else walked in at all hours, not just the increasingly sociable Jack, so he is trapped in here with me when he visits, until I send him home. More than once these experimental, tentative weeks together he has awakened suddenly from a nap, immediately become frantic and run for the (closed) door, or started wailing when I went up to sleep and forgot to release him. *Let me out of here.*

Jack wants to try some connection, but he wants to remain in charge; to be free and also feel the warmth of another creature (and not one whose neck he is wringing). Don't we all? Good luck with that, Jack. But as he adapts to my invasion, my flabby, formless "schedule" gains another marker, not just teatime and Garbage Night, but a third to-do that's becoming more reliably timed: *Feed the cat.* I'm really gaining on the creating-structure thing; the week is taking shape.

Are you suggesting taking our relationship to the next level? I ask Jack, just in from an overnight of hunting, while doling out his kibble, explaining that this is not a good time for me (all of this, of course, out loud). Conventional wisdom says not to get involved when something life altering has just happened, Jack; to wait six months minimum. Yes, I say, yes, Jackie, yes, my dear Potentate, I know I handed over all that money to the professional matchmaker to find me a companion (and help me tick off Item Number 4 on the Passion Test list, the one that rose to Number 3 on the second pass, the item about all that great sex).

You are a cat, Jack (and *I am not a cat person*), and as for the matchmaker's candidates so far: No, no thank you, anyway; I just want my heating pad and my roasted brussels sprouts and for *The Wire* and *MI-5* in particular never to end, and to be alone. *Can't you understand, Jack? Alone. The way you used to like to be, too.* Alone in the woods, like in Andre's cartoon. Alone, the way I have frequently been warned against, perhaps: risking isolation, even hermitage, as has been my lifelong inclination.

Mr. Right will not fly in the window, Margaret.

Dr. Goudard always used to say that to me in the early years together, when I would hole up instead of joining up; go home and crash (oops, another aviation / avian pun) instead of dusting myself off, putting on a fresh coat of lipstick, and staging a fully engaged and meaningful social life at the workday's end.

Network I did not, ever, neither personally nor professionally, though despite this failing, this outsiderism of my loner nature, there was plenty of air traffic to control (or lose control of): some Mr. Rights, though not any Mr. Forevers, and the occasional Mr. Wrong—including a wildly charismatic pilot once, who proved my undoing, though his arrival was also the most delightfully satisfying thing I ever threw back in Dr. Goudard's face:

Look what flew through my metaphoric window, Cheese. Look. You said it couldn't happen.

Right now, I am content to find myself with the bluebirds and with the pine grosbeaks, hoping that before the latter head back north someone else will fly in to entertain me, but from a comfortable distance. Yes, I know; Emily Dickinson: *Hope is the thing with feathers.*

I SUPPOSE I HAVE ALWAYS BEEN A TAD HIGH GEAR. Consider the source:

The prefix *Mar-* has been a persistent, insistent sound in my life. I am named for a Grandma Margaret I never met; am granddaughter to another I revered, Marion; I am big sister to a Marion, too; best friend to a Marco; ex-lieutenant to a Martha. I am regularly called all of those names (except Marco, owing to gender realities), and answer to them by reflex. If you utter that first critical syllable, I will turn my head or come running before you form the next.

That is not to say I am obedient. I was taught very good

manners, but they fail when something strikes me as wrong. Then I have trouble stifling myself about it—especially around family. In dysfunctional-family-speak, I was the Confronter.

My parents were liberals, though Daddy (also known as Podners) retained his Republican Party registration. One afternoon on a beach in the Florida Keys, when we were very small, my mother pointed to someone in the distance. "That's Richard Nixon, and he's a very bad man," she said sternly. He was Eisenhower's VP at the time, I suppose.

These two very smart, very appealing, very mismatched people surrounded us with books and exposed us to large doses of travel, music, museums, the theater. We had to see everything, and from good seats. Our regular after-theater dinner place was the legendary Toots Shor's, and we called the bigger-than-life New York City saloonkeeper Uncle Toots. I don't think this was a place many other people in our neighborhood took their kids. To this day, I hate Broadway shows and especially musicals; my Mar- sister and my Mar- best friend will both gleefully belt out the lyrics to any show tune you ask of them. I still know a few myself, but prefer to hope the echoes will go away. No chance, probably, since my sister taught her Chinese-born baby girl to sing "You Can't Get a Man with a Gun" as soon as Grace could string together a phrase. Quite a departure from Ethel Merman's rendition or stage presence, shall we say.

My (very loosely speaking) "godfather" was a famous trainer of racehorses. Many things were *very loosely speaking* in our upbringing and in our parents' marriage, actually: My mother wore blue, not a wedding gown, and they had lunch, not a reception; Marion has no godfather; and neither of us has a middle name. We were not baptized until Grandma Marion finally won out when I was four and Marion two, and they walked us down the aisle together. Lordy.

My parents didn't belong to churches. Then the guilt of raising two heathens set in. Off we went. Like I said, Lordy. I was the kid who tortured Pastor Auman nonstop with the one obnoxious question: *How do you know for sure?* One Sunday morning before church, around age fifteen, I fell off the stool in front of my bedroom "dressing table" while curling my eyelashes, pulling out all the top ones on one eye. (They grow back. God is forgiving, even to impertinent nonbelievers.)

I was sent away various summers to various places: Girl Scout Camp (where I fell out of a platform tent, rolled down a hill, and broke my wrist); private girls' camp in New Hampshire (where I was humiliated to be the only girl in my cabin or perhaps the whole camp whose mother hadn't bought her a bra yet); Cape Cod with our parents' most bohemian friends, whose one girl among their five kids was my best grade-school friend, Stephanie.

On Cape Cod, I learned the word *phosphorescent* (owing to jellyfish you could see at night); danced with much older boys in my maroon Indian-print Nehru jacket to Jimi Hendrix; and painted my friend's mother's aging refrigerator yellow with abstract, flower-power flourishes (in oil, as in permanently). We were perhaps thirteen years old. My sister (aka Not the Confronter) never went to camp (or Cape Cod). She stayed home and played sports all summer long with Mommy, or so I imagine, since I was not present to witness it.

My father was a sports editor, with access to Mickey Mantle and Muhammad Ali and all manner of box seats, every boychild's dream. His first marriage, at age forty-five to my mother (then twenty-four), resulted in two girls, me first. I don't think he minded one bit, and a lot of neighborhood boys got great perks. Marion and I were popular as a result.

Girl Scouts, Barbie dolls, and trolls played a probably alarming but critical role until well into my teens, though not Marion's. (I later horrified my poor sister by bringing a pink Barbie van as a gift to my niece's third birthday. I was the way-most-popular adult at the party among the kids, but apparently my sister hadn't intended to raise a Barbie-playing daughter. *Oops.*)

My mother got rid of all my dolls of both kinds without asking, but I still have my sash from Troop 4–334. The embroidered badges on it include ones for sports and sewing. Even today, this strikes me as funny. (No, I do not wear the sash; I keep it folded with my table linens in the sideboard.)

Re: sports: I do not participate in sports contests of any kind, since falling facedown on a tennis court as the boy I loved watched on. "Poetry in motion," another boy yelled through the fence. Love–15, and no match. Re: sewing: When I stood up at the bell signaling the end of sewing shop one afternoon in junior high, the project we were making was stitched to my skirt. I had to wear it, collagelike, to my next class.

I did not drink until I was forty, or at least didn't except once, at a "boy-girl party" in my best friend's basement, where I sipped several kinds of wine that kids had smuggled in (think Thunderbird and Mateus Rosé). I promptly became dizzy, and threw up on the shoes of the boy I loved then (the one before the boy I loved in the tennis incident).

Our mother was quite athletic, a lifetime sailor and tennis player, as is my sister, who also excels in just about anything with a bat, ball, racquet, or net involved. Re: sailing: Though I was a competitive swimmer as a kid, and do not fear the water whatsoever, I am happier on dry land, and never wanted to sail. Being on, but not in, the water makes no sense to me. Being firmly planted suits me best of all.

"Nonsense," said my mother, signing me up for sailing lessons at the local dock. The sadistic young instructor paired me with Jane, the other most-terrified pupil, and hoisted our mainsail then cast the two of us adrift from our mooring when we refused to set sail ourselves. Learn by doing? No chance; we lay clinging to the floorboards, crying, as the boat bobbed around the bay, the big sail slack and flapping to punctuate our sobs. Apparently someone ran up the hill to the tennis club and got my mother, but my memory remains fixed on the being cast adrift part, so I do not know what happened next. Ask my sister.

People say I am a picky eater. My father cooked our Monday dinners (his day off) from Craig Claiborne, Pierre Franey, even the giant brown encyclopedia *Larousse Gastronomique*. My mother relied on her aluminum Mirro electric frypan as an all-purpose vessel in which to create weekly installments of chicken cacciatore, meatballs (served with spaghetti that was thankfully not cooked in the frypan), and banana pancakes. A modern WASP housewife.

As a counterpoint to that characterization, my sister will tell you about a dish she calls "Mommy's rosemary chicken." The secret ingredient in Mommy's rosemary chicken was crumbled potato chips. There are few things that don't taste good to kids "breaded" in potato chips; even our family dinner table scene brightened on such nights. (The recipe is actually our grandmother Marion's, however, and I have the recipe card in her uptight nineteenth-century penmanship to prove it.) My sister and I rinsed off most of our entrées en route from stovetop to table (not said rosemary chicken). We feared coming into contact with what we called "juice spots," those bits of coagulated meat drippings of an unusual texture that make good starter for gravy. In what is perhaps a related development: I have been a vegetarian for more than thirty years.

I am not crazy about ice cream, which I think is because I was searching in my mother's wallet for money for a Good Humor when I found a photo of my father's close friend, a man well known to me, instead. We vacationed with his family, and his son was my sister's first crush; we ate dinner with them at least once a week. We did everything with him (and apparently "everything" was really *everything*). I was nine years old, and it didn't make sense, and also made total sense.

In the instant that hand touched photo, I was forced to grasp the concept of adultery and became the Confronter. *Tag: You're it*. No longer someone searching for a dollar, I began my life's search for an honest answer, no matter how ugly or inconvenient. And I began a lifetime habit of asking questions, endless questions—*Who am I if I am not mroach@marthastewart dot com any longer?* is just the latest of a lengthy string. The first big one of my life was spoken silently to myself, there in that bedroom.

"Why is there a picture of Jack in Mommy's wallet?" I did not keep silent for long.

The answers—from Mommy, from Daddy, and even from Marion, simply trying to behave as she was told—were always the same: *Be quiet*, they'd say, in one form or another. *Don't talk that way. Be quiet.*

That moment ended the simplicity of early sisterhood for me and Marion—creating our first rift that was not our rift at all but a hand-me-down, the way it happens when children inherit disagreements and not just freckles and asthma. It was a divide that would stay with us for decades, and a discovery that would send the young Confronter into the high gear that she is still working to subdue. *Down, agitator, down.*

It was yoga that eventually silenced my agitator—a yogic breath or two, the closing of my eyes and settling into even a short practice, and I was still, or getting there. But somewhere on the road north I have lost my yoga, and I never get so hungry for human companionship as I do thirst for this most Beloved of all lovers, my practice, to return.

I had big plans: In anticipation of my full-time rural residence, and in recognition of how tiny my house really is (particularly obvious when you are outstretching both arms or extending them overhead in expansive gestures of openness and devotion), I built a yoga room above my new small barn. In the planning and negotiating stages for my great escape, this is where I had imagined I would be each morning, before settling down to some new creative and fulfilling work. Heaven, and the thought that made me brave when any steps in the gradual and complicated unhooking of all the lines got intimidating. I haven't been in the supposed studio so far these four months, and I keep telling myself it's just the winter that makes it unappealing—having to go turn on the heat and let it warm up beforehand, the extra slippery steps required this time of year. That's why I am not using my yoga space. *Winter.*

Or maybe I need the sense of community, the spirit of a *sangha*, to light my fire. I have collected all the schedules from yoga centers within thirty minutes of here, read the teacher bios, made my way to one and then another—only to never return again. Yes, there was the unfortunate first try: a class with the half-naked instructor (what did he stuff into those tiny elastic shorts—*is that a codpiece?*) and the Céline Dion music that I should have run screaming from; that's why I am not doing yoga, I had a bad experience, *I need time to recover from that hour and a half.* And then there was the class that was too strenuous (*I need something easier, it has been a while*); the one that was too simple (*I am bored*); the one that was too crowded, and on and on.

I have lost my yoga. My yoga has been a casualty of these first months; or had I lost it gradually in the run-up to the new life? It's so much easier to blame Céline Dion, and go watch DVDs under the covers. Maybe with a glass of wine. Monkey mind is soothed by this combination, I am finding with increasing frequency, or at least it is quieted for a few hours at a time.

Melting, Not Meltdown

Spring is coming; I can smell it. March and often much of April are the oddest of times: delightful, and also disgusting. The putrid rankness of dairy slurry being hauled from the collection pits and spread about the fields hangs in the damp air, a top note mingling with the base note of smoke from nonstop burning of brush and leaf piles. Recycling of various forms is going on all around me; this is how we welcome spring on my farming road, in the place where I now live every single day.

I have always marveled that you cannot smell it indoors; how can the walls of this little house—now, with the new siding installed, as well as years ago, with all those extra layers cob-jobbed onto one another—actually act as a barrier to so insistent a brew of odors? But you cannot. Hallelujah that apparently indoors just smells like me, a scent I cannot pick up on or describe, owing to our animal origins that let us smell the other but remain free of too much olfactory distraction of ourselves. Insulated indoors thus, the outdoor aroma of coming spring takes on the status of a stealth weapon, and I am always startled: knocked back when I open the door to go out foraging for sticks and stones, the first permitted task of each almost-garden season.

Long before people can get out and around and navigate the thawing soil, the tankage is set free.

It is a smell I hate, and also love; a smell of coming freedom; a scent like when the man you lust after is sweaty-dirty, but on him it smells good, at least to you. You want—and need—to take it in up close, with the hungry nose of an animal. This gardener lusts after her filthy lover, the spring, even when it is foul and tests her.

Soon we will all be allowed out again with regularity, to stretch our legs after the long, cramped ride that is winter here. But for now, just the occasional adventure to pick up sticks and stones is possible, and even that is not allowed if the ground has gone all loose and squishy and we are deep in mud season, the other trick that March and April play, putting a girl on one more kind of slippery footing. *Come hither, my dear, and get stuck in the mire we've whipped up for you.*

Add it to my list of safety rules: *Never walk on sodden turf or soil.* In this case the peril or lack of safety is not to me, exactly, but to the particles of clay and sand and silt that are my foundation as a gardener, and of my life on earth. On those days when the soil is still firm enough from frost or has drained off well enough between progressive thaws and intermittent rains, and on those days only, I pick up sticks, breathing in the festering, fuming smells of this prelude to the imminent, urgent new season.

Of course, I know even while I collect the debris exactly what will happen next: I wait for the wind to start, and for the heavens to deposit another supply of brush onto the temporarily tidy ground, the ground I have just cleared, as if on cue. Clean the slate, and then clean it again. Continue without complaint or else you will be back where you started twenty years or more ago: up to your waist in the stuff, needing to clear the land again and burn a fire so big and bright that it will last for days, and your hair will stink of smoke, as will what you are now calling clothing, each through many washings afterward. It is too late in life to start again from scratch (*oh, god, did I really just write that?*), so I gather branches and twigs, keep things tidy, something *oh please something* must feel within my control, a rhythm, *five-six, pick up sticks; seven-eight, lay them straight.*

The ice is melting on the frog ponds, their surfaces a yin-yang of frozen-unfrozen on top now, more water (the dark portion) showing than just the glimpse that the deicer had kept open these last months. On favorable days, the largest of the bullfrogs climbs up onto the solid part (the white of the ice), moving like a dinosaur in that slo-mo, lumbering way of old sci-fi movies or cartoons, his thunder thighs engineering steps so deliberate that it looks as if a single one might shake the ground and register a vast release of seismic energy. Then he has a look around—now he is more a sea lion on a glacier, dressed in his dark brown winter color with his big belly draped on the ice—and, apparently unimpressed, plods back underneath the surface to zone out a while longer. Nothing much buzzing by yet that's worth eating alive, I suppose; *catch you later.*

Earlier, a flock of American robins—not the same *Turdus migratorius* individuals that are here in the fairer months, probably, but their look-alike cousins, from up the road apiece, I bet, but you can never really tell—were enjoying the hole in the frogs' pool, frolicking like it was Friday at five fifteen PM in one of the bars perched on the upper balconies in Grand Central Terminal. *Drinks all around!*

The big old clematis on the porch posts are a mess, blowing about all brittle and dry in the wind, and about this time I always wonder why I left them standing, sparing them a fall haircut. But like everything here there is a balancing act, a silver lining: The dark-eyed juncos (*Junco hyemalis*), a kind of sparrow who joins me in large numbers in the cooler months, seem to love the seeds that scatter.

On these same favorable days, Jack seems to know something is up, too, and as the last snow melts he revels in the increasing choices of hunting targets, picking his spots outdoors to watch, to wait. Chipmunks run at high speed from end to end of the various stone walls out back, stopping midway along their favorite fieldstone stretch, the one behind the bigger of the two frog ponds. They ascend the three-foot-tall Indonesian bust of Buddha I placed there years ago and sit awhile, sit right there on Buddha's *ushnisha*, the cranial bump symbolizing the expanded wisdom that the prince Siddhartha Gautama attained with his Buddhahood. At the moment of enlightenment, the prince was attended by birds and also by snakes—each species in that tale so-called twice-borns, having hatched from eggs—but here the serpents, at least, have not yet deemed the temperatures to their liking, and remain in hiding.

Jack eyes the chippies, knocking off one for sport from time to time, but they are not good eating; he delivers them to me whole. Where he gets some of the other things that he leaves in a diffuse slurry of reddish tones on the back porch I do not know; whose parts they once were eludes me, too, but now Jack wants them to be mine. *I love you, Mommy.* Porchkill.

Spring is coming, and everyone is feeling homicidal, or unloading their old shit.

I AM TIRED OF MY OLD SHIT, TOO, but I am not so deluded to believe that it would enrich the soil if I just opened the window and tossed it all out there, or that anyone would welcome it being delivered to their doorstep. For my part in the enactment under way, I am trying to stay focused on life, and progress; on forward momentum—on those elusive concepts of rhythm and structure that I seem to have left behind 120 miles to the south. I should have hooked the bungee cords on better to that part of my pickup-load of possessions brought along here for the ride, but *thwack! boing!* (there goes rhythm; good-bye, structure). Off they seem to have popped, releasing any sense of order.

Some days, the mud is relenting and so I get to investigate and explore, and before long I find myself busy waiting: for the graceful, native woodland perennial called blue cohosh, *Caulophyllum thalictroides*, to push its reddish-green shoots up through the soil; for the *Dicentra spectabilis*, or bleeding heart, to emerge all flushed in purply pinks; for the species peonies to push through the crust in near-psychedelic shades, too. Fall does not have a corner on the fiery pigments called anthocyanins; tender new plants use them to trick and ward off predatory her-bivores (*I'm not green, so you don't want to eat me!*) and to give the you-sexy-thing look to arriving or awakening pollinators (*Whoa, baby, check it out! Want to do it?*).

Learn something new every day.

I have become a keen observer of plant sex, and know that nonstop bird sex is up next on the program, once all the players fly into the theater ready to perform. (Item Number 3 on my Passion Test, Version 2, remains unresolved, in case anybody is keeping track.) So I am investigating the out of doors, looking for signs. What is the cohosh waiting for? As I know I have already mentioned (do I sound desperate yet?), I am waiting for things to happen, for sure signs of life as I crawl around the leaf litter these tenaciously cold days, uncovering possibilities, trying not to leave a footprint or kneeprint in my wake, avoiding forensic evidence of my restlessness, my impatience. What am I hoping to find? Things like the fiercely alive, sharpened-looking shoots of hostas would help. The undeniable beginning to the garden year would hold a special delight for me this time around: Perhaps it could be my time clock, the one I so need to organize the days and weeks and months that still feel shapeless.

Another week or two passes and I have shifted its focus if not its intent, always skipping ahead to the next moment with half my attention. I am waiting for the first bunch of homegrown tulips to set on the dining table, but so far all I have is foliage and some emerging buds. I am sure the cutting tulips will fail; I say so every year at this time—*no buds, why no buds?* The blue cohosh and those sharp little hosta shoots appeared out of nowhere, finally, along with a dozen other things, a landslide of awakening that starts with *Galanthus* and quickly ricochets across the yard and back again to *Eranthis-Helleborus-Salix-Daphne-Chionodoxa-Narcissus-Acer-Corylopsis-Magnolia-Lindera.* And that is just one week. Causes for optimism; yes, I can live on Plant Time—their comings will fill the empty appointment book, along with entries for mow and rake and divide and prune.

I know, I know: From here on out it will all happen fast, maybe too fast, and then I will be regretting instead of waiting. Even once you have your first tulips for cutting, your blue cohosh, and all the rest, there's forever something that hasn't happened yet that holds a special promise. Like maybe some rain, or at other times that the rain finally stops?

Finally, then, to underscore the powerlessness—the root of all that longing that makes you kneel in the dirt, as if to pray—the reminder comes, slam across the forehead: Nothing lasts. Not winter, nor spring, nor any other season; not *Narcissus* nor magnolias. Not us. The Japanese celebrate this very fact (instead of fearing it) in the form of the *Sakura Matsuri*, or Cherry Blossom Festival, which honors the ephemeral nature of all things. Picnics take place under the trees as the blossoms pass peak and let go their pink precipitation, which melts and melds into pink pools on the ground beneath the very trees that failed to hold the petals back from their insistent flight. *Yippee! Things have fallen apart; cause for celebration!*

I like to celebrate impermanence at every passing in the garden, like the day in April when the magnolia flowers shatter in the warm breeze and fall from heaven to earth, like snow... speaking of things that are transient. But even for one with my generally agreeable disposition on the subject of impermanence, this year is feeling a little too unstructured, a little too loose to really grasp. *(Did I just say* grasp? *Oh, dear. Still grasping. Oh, dear.)*

I am wishing more each day now that my yoga had stuck

around. I will not know how much I wish that until the relentless run of violent electrical storms begins. It won't be long.

THE LIGHT HERE IS REALLY SOMETHING, emphasis on thing. It has a life of its own, a personality; it's a force. And it comes in colors.

Over here in my corner of the Earth, out my window where my gaze is fixed whenever my eyes are open, I call it the godlight, because there's no explaining otherwise; that slanted light that makes elongated, high-drama shadows and turns everything warm and glowing, defying even this nonbeliever's nonfaith. Note: This light is nondenominational, hence the lowercase *g*. All are welcome to witness it, and be bathed in it. It is my most precious companion, my one Beloved who remains, with yoga gone.

More biblical still is the local version of lightning, and though all are similarly welcome to witness its special majesty, most won't care to, I suspect. I know that I do not; bring on the godlight, but damn the lightning. *I am so afraid.*

There's iron, you see, in them there hills all around me, and like Mr. Parker of the century-old children's book *Tom Swift Among the Diamondmakers*, part of the Tom Swift series by Victor Appleton, I blame the iron for fueling my brontophobia or keraunophobia or astraphobia or tonitrophobia, whichever it is really called. *(How can I be afraid of something that doesn't even have a clear name?)* Well, Appleton's 1911 character was:

"There's a mass of iron ore there!" yelled Mr. Parker.
"The lightning is attracted to it!... We are in the midst of

the storm!...We are standing on a mass of iron ore! Any minute may be our last!"

And that is how it feels several days a week here this first spring of my supposed freedom: This may be my new beginning, but any minute may also be my last, my rebirth by fire (or will it be a sizzling-hot death?). The incoming storms are more frequent than in memory, and so early; not waiting for the muggy, despairing days of late summer to erupt in violence, but staging brutal performances each week as spring tries angrily to take hold. There were even some electrical outbursts in the heaviest snows of winter, I recall now; a forecast, I suppose, of oddities currently upon me. Encore after encore, though I was never applauding. Apparently the claps of thunder were being heard as approval and encouragement by the lightning: *Bravo!*

"Is that lightning?" I said one night at dinner with friends, in a "local" restaurant about thirty minutes from home. Though seated with my back to the glass storefront, I thought I had caught a momentary shift in the light—I got that flashback feeling lightning always triggers, pulling as it does at my viscera and my very soul. Lightning it was.

What I fear more than being under the dining table is having to drive through lightning storms to get to the dining table. In all the weekend years, I'd driven over one or another of the dips and swells in the Taconic State Parkway right into many massive storms, the kind that seem to light up the sky a little too long to be real—or to signal anything but the end of the world. Right at me they would seem to come, in daring pursuit, leaving no out but to keep driving toward Copake Falls.

On the way back from that dinner, I became absolutely frantic, gripping the wheel and screwing up my face in that wincing way, fearing the next bolt but looking more like it had already hit. At Hillsdale, about the halfway mark and the only place with an actual crossroads of business activity—read: two open gas stations—I stopped to gather myself. I also stopped because I could see where the storm was at that moment. As usual, it was pulsing most vividly right over Copake Falls, home to my table-as-shelter.

And so I waited, afraid, even, to go inside the convenience store—too wrung out to walk the fifteen feet to the doors and the glassed-in fluorescent haven beyond. Once I could take in my temporary shelter in the storm, I saw that I was not alone: Life had been going on around me all the while that I sat lost in fear. Cars were arriving, pulling into spots; out of them got a woman in search of a half gallon of milk, or a man with a cigarette quickly vaporizing between his fingers and needing another pack fast. Two young women climbed down from a big pickup beside me and stood talking right out in the charged air, talking about a band they like—one more enthusiastically than the other—and about what they have to do tomorrow. They did not seem to even notice the show of nature's enormous power around them.

My neighbors, apparently, are immune to what ails me, or so it seems. And I, raised in the flatlands of suburban New York City, seem to have skipped that all-important inoculation. Damn.

Thunder and lightning: Since it is technically impossible to have one without the other (lightning causes thunder, even if you are too far away to hear the latter clatter), even the phobias defining such fears lump the two. But I am scared of the lightning, not the noise; morbidly, irrationally afraid of the great pulses of electrostatic energy, each a hundred million to a billion volts, and containing billions of watts.

Yes, I am afraid of energy like this that heats the air to 18,000 degrees Fahrenheit and even up to 60,000; afraid of something that strikes the ground in the United States approximately 25 million times each year, making my chance of being struck in any given year about one in 240,000 (by National Weather Service estimates). Assuming an average life span of eighty years, they calculate, my lifetime probability becomes one in three thousand, and in case I was not uncomfortable enough, they go a step further to extrapolate that the chances of someone close to me being struck is one in three hundred, assuming we each have a circle of about ten family and closest friends. (Or at least have them until they are each struck by lightning.)

How close is a close call? I am calculating as I sit beneath the trestle-style farm table that is my dining-surface-turned-desk. In this house with its many tall, equal-and-opposite windows (and no shades or curtains), there is little refuge; the enclosed stairwell is my only other hideaway, and in there I sit if the storms set themselves against the dark background of night, a hellish chiaroscuro painted by the heavens. How close was *that one*? Count the seconds between the flash and the bang, and divide by five (because sound travels about one mile in five seconds) to determine the answer in miles. How close? *Close.* Like all of the sieges lately, so close that even Jack the hunter, Jack the formerly wild thing from the woods, the warrior, is frantic, diving beneath the table with me, uttering ungodly sounds. We have both fallen so far. *Close.*

I have studied all this lately—*learn something new every day*—hoping to find something that would relieve my whatever-you-want-to-call-it phobia, but all it did was make things worse. (A little knowledge is a dangerous thing? Or is it just that lightning is in fact as dangerous as it looks, and feels?)

I have never been as fearful before now, though, nor has it seemed so frequent nor so powerful. I have apparently landed my already somewhat radarless, rudderless ship in lightning alley. What should I do, Tom Swift?

And while I am under the table so many afternoons lately, I realize that it is all my fault, these louder and louder signals.

Because I did not listen to myself, they sent the birds.

Because I did not listen to the birds, they sent the frogs.

Because I did not listen to the frogs, they sent the cat.

Because I did not listen to the cat, they sent the relentless lightning.

And now I live here with all of them.

Oh, and yes, the snakes: These hills are full of them, too. By all means, bring on the writhing, rattling snakes.

Reptiles and amphibians are grouped in most of my reference books, so when I want to look up some welcome frog or other who's just shown himself for the first time of the new season these gently warming days as spring comes on, the section of color plates inevitably falls open to you-know-who. I try to force myself to look at the rich-toned color illustrations and photographs, spread by spread, species by species; a visual antivenin to take away the painful reaction to even the sight of illustrated snakes, let alone the real slithering thing. I try to read about them, too; though never late in the day, when it will only fuel more snake dreams (like this one from 1991):

Three giant hognosed snakes, a set of small, medium, and large live specimens, are hanging on the bedroom wall above my headboard. Someone who in the dream I understand is going to sleep over suggests that we move the bed out from the wall, away from the hanging snakes. We do, and it reveals a hole by the baseboard, which I quickly stuff with Brillo pads, using a butter knife that appeared from nowhere for the task.

Snakes. Most have only one serious lung (the left one vestigial or even absent in many species); I have had weeks when I felt like that, such as my times in the hospital with the punctures. Legless, eyelidless, silent, skin-shedding, carnivorous reptiles. Snakes.

Learn something new every day.

These are animals whose skulls are so loosely articulated that they can bite off a lot, and actually take it all in. In fact, they swallow it whole. Having chewed on many an emotional meal a bit too long in my life, I envy that last powerful decisiveness, but I still hate snakes. (Dare I say: *I am not a snake person*? Will they soon be on a pillow beside my writing chair many hours a day, snoring, the way once-wild Jack is now? Is this where we are all headed, all into the house-as-ark?)

I have known since my second year of weekending, once Herb and I were regular Sunday morning sit-on-the-stoop friends, that we have eastern timber rattlesnakes here; like every other lifetime local resident, Herb has his share of snake stories (many of which conclude with the kicker, "Tastes like chicken.").

"What's in the back of your truck?" I asked one day, shortly after the fire instruction, noticing the lump wrapped carefully in a tarp. "Rattler," he said, and then the punch line that I would come to be able to predict, followed by a wry Herb smile. He knew he had a suggestible flatlander's attention, even that early on.

I know from the books I force-fed myself in very small spoonfuls to try to take the fear down a level that from mid-October or so through sometime in April, for about seven months a year, these ectotherms help one another stay warm by huddling in groups in one of the various hibernacula above me apiece, some rocky den in a crevice of which there are many at higher spots in these there hills (the hills that also seem to be a lightning magnet; what in the world ever drew me here again?). There may be ten or sixty or even a hundred snakes together in a single hibernaculum, and copperheads—another venomous local species—may join the winterlong sleepover, too.

If that were not creepy enough, when it is warm, the male timber rattler is a lone predator; he migrates farthest from the den in summertime, meaning potentially into my world, onto my recycled-tire welcome mat. You already know how that part of the story goes, the part about my left foot.

Flash of backstory: I credit Grandma Marion, mother to my mother, for my love of nature—but not because she was an outdoorsy type herself, exactly—or maybe she was at a younger age, who knows; we didn't meet until she was into her sixties, as my mother was a late-life baby, her only child. Yes, she gardened with the best of the Douglaston Garden Club ladies, growing prize yellow irregular-incurve chrysanthemum standards that she could also arrange with ribbon-winning flair. But to my knowledge, her animal interactions were limited to the family fox terrier, a backyard flock of bantam hens that my mother helped her tend as a girl, and this one particularly giant black snake that Grandma came upon in the basement, curled up inside a piece of outdoor pottery she'd stored there for the off-season. I know the feeling.

Yes, Grandma gave me more than just her genes; she handed down the snake juju. *Gonna tell a story morning glory all about the serpentine fire.*

Whenever I talk or write about *Crotalus horridus* or any other snake, I wring my hands and feel the need to move fast on to the next topic, please. Can we just keep moving; can he (that snake) please move on? *Is it November yet?* Or must I, the gardener, hibernate all through the summertime in my one-woman hibernaculum to avoid him (she types, wringing hands between keystrokes)? This is not Texas or Arizona; why are there rattlesnakes?

Perhaps Jonathan will know.

IT IS LATE SUMMER 2008. I am jobless; my consulting contract with Martha has ended. I do not qualify for unemployment benefits, I learn, because I carefully followed tax law and my accountant's thoughtful advice and incorporated my new life on January 1, becoming Margaret Roach Inc., and therefore I am technically employed, although the company is revenue-less. The print media industry (where my skills are centered and where I could presumably have supported myself with ongoing consulting, as was the plan) is already on bad times, and the first rumblings of more economic trouble are registering semiconsciously.

Okay, Plan B: I call my long-ago book agent and say I need

to come up with some form of work. She (never one to mince words) says, "Give me a few things and we'll throw them all up against the wall and see—you're too old to bank on only one thing, so let's try a few." As she says *too old* I think *ouch*, but all I can conjure is Felix throwing that plate of linguini (that Oscar had incorrectly called spaghetti) up against the wall, after Oscar asked him to please get it off his poker table. "Now it's garbage," Felix says. I need to do better than garbage—and in triplicate, apparently, and pronto.

The proposal, at least, is al dente, apparently. In October, there is a book contract, just in the nick, personally and globally; I can stall dipping into savings awhile longer. By November, it starts to sound like nobody will offer another contract for anything anywhere in the world ever again, in any industry, and then some: Summertime's $50 tanks of gas have turned to the $85 billion AIG bailout and then the proclamation of the "once-in-a-century credit tsunami" by Greenspan. (I look for hope, and anything soothing-sounding, in all this: Perhaps I was a genius to leave the corporate world before the linguini hit the fan, I tell myself daily, a tactic aimed at dispelling the latest fear trying to set up shop in my head, to root where there is simply no room for such invasives.) Though the first payment on a book advance doesn't come close to paying the bills—unless I write very, very fast, more at a clip like Barbara Cartland's, who dictated a romance novel a week—and the savings that were meant to yield a little to make up the difference just shrank a lot, I quickly spend a chunk of it. Shades of past Saks binges, or stroke of genius?

I am blaming the reptiles, and now the book, and also Jonathan Ellerby, whom I have not seen in several years but am now conducting a one-woman manhunt for. It is Jonathan to whom I have, in my slightly unnerved mind, assigned the magical power to help me find the way into the book and out of the snake pit (oh, wait, I already left the old life, didn't I?). So even before that first check arrives I commit a piece of it to pay for a stay at a luxury spa, the nearby Berkshires outpost of Canyon Ranch, which Jonathan turns out to be coming to from their Tucson headquarters to host a program later this year. He has become the resort's spirituality director in the years since we walked in the Arizona desert picking up stones and role-playing with them. I not only found my man, but he is being delivered to me, just minutes from my door, and soon.

It's a sign, I tell myself. (I know, I am spending far too much time alone; yes, believe me, I know.)

I sign up; to hell with the money. This is not the moment to start taking on the fear of going broke, just when I am trying to face the terrors I already have, plenty for one person with two thirds or more of her days behind her—just when I mere months ago faced what I thought was the biggest fear of all: letting go of one's career and with it the source of not just income but also esteem.

And, I tell myself, this really isn't as bad as those fifteen-minute fashion binges—it's part of the research for the book, isn't it; maybe *the corporation* should send me on assignment? Or something; *note to self: call accountant*. I keep telling myself anything that sounds soothing, and usually aloud, the pitch of my utterances now betraying an edge that wasn't there in Month 1.

Between the date I register and the date I arrive, the fact that the world is coming to an economic end is outed in increasingly unbearable tidbits, headline by headline. I could cancel, and keep my deposit on credit for a moment when times seem better. But I haven't been getting out much lately, not even to the post office to pick up my mail more than once every four or five days, now that I think of it, and those outings are usually with a jacket thrown over whatever I slept in, and absent not just makeup, but also those all-important earrings. Lately I have been under house arrest, but not the kind anyone imposes except yourself. My schedule is so loose that it defies the very word, more gaseous than solid. I need connection, and human contact, so off I go, up the road about forty minutes, to Lenox, Massachusetts, to check myself in.

I have been here many times, disappearing impulsively whenever I got so angry or brittle at work that I could not do one more day of the corporate-executive charade without bursting wide open. But this visit is different. It is eerie when I arrive at the Ranch, as they refer to it, built on the site of and incorporating the former Bellefontaine Mansion, one of the Berkshires' finest estates from an era long gone, erected in 1897 as a copy of Louis XIV's Petit Trianon at Versailles. In fact, it's not just eerie, but downright embarrassing.

Everyone seems to be aware of the now-double anachronism, not just the way a modern restaurant and spa complex, with its characterless, peach-heavy dentist-office paint palette, has been connected to the historic marble and brick building rich with detail—that's always the oddball nature of the Ranch. Now there's another layer of contradiction, in just the fact of our being there while everywhere around us, we all fall down. Headlines from newspapers set out on the leather ottomans by the fireplaces tell us the grim facts. Will people really go to places like this ever again? It feels a bit like a voyage on the *Titanic*. And the band played on.

But I am here where there is no wine and lots of yoga, and I am here for Jonathan, for more of his block capital letters on the backs of copious handouts; for the light and sparkle that I tell myself bounces off him even when the topic is as dark as snakes. I have done much crazier things, and wasted money and time more foolishly (or so I hope proves true).

I need to write the book to get to the next check, and most important on the larger scale, the psychic one, to get all these thoughts out of me that I have sequestered for so long while being in service to another. So essentially here I am, paying a luxury resort money to have a doctor of comparative religion—a former hospital chaplain in turquoise beads who is in their employ (and also many years my junior)—tell my own story back to me, or at least his interpretation of it. Hear my confession, won't you, brother?

And talk back to me he does, and then some. He seems to remember our conversations of earlier years; I don't have to explain why I left the city or any of it, really. *Aren't we clever?* All I say to provoke Jonathan is the brief introductory paragraph as we begin our reunion: that I quit my job, moved to my garden, and spend a lot of time staring at, and yes, talking to, frogs and birds—and worrying about snakes, *particularly like the one I almost stepped on in July, Jonathan, a really giant rattlesnake, you know?*

The divine doctor speaks:

"You have a shamanic way of seeing the world, Margaret," he says, "but why do you have such a resistance to stepping into the metaphysics of nature—to accepting that you are a gatekeeper of it? In the shamanic world, it's not a choice to be a gatekeeper; you just are."

Say what?

Just as quietly and matter-of-factly, as if we are talking about matter-of-fact things any child would understand, he continues:

"You are willing to connect to the science of nature, of your garden plants and the creatures in your environment, but not the psychological dimension. Frogs, birds, snakes—they are all aligned, don't you see? The frogs and birds—they are liminal creatures, Margaret, like you: They live, and move, between worlds. And snakes are all about the transformational." Twice-borns, every one.

And then the clincher:

"If we honor our gifts, Margaret, awareness will arrive, and we can live with more congruency, closer to our true self. Pay attention to the signs, as they say."

Because I didn't listen to the snakes, they sent Jonathan—and a large American Express bill shortly thereafter.

I am sent "home" that evening to my oversize, overdecorated guest room with notes and a handwritten list of books that I must read, but I am most of all intent on reading up about this new word, or at least new to my ears: *liminal* (from the Latin word *limen*, for threshold). Yes: I am betwixt and between, neither here nor there, I am liminal but not in the way I was for far too achingly long before I pointed the Saab and myself in the other (the right?) direction. This is another threshold altogether. Onward. Please tell me I am making progress, someone.

And when Jonathan said "shamanistic," was he meaning witch doctor or what, exactly? The only shamans I know about are the medicine men a couple of plant-loving ethnobotanist friends work with in the Amazon and elsewhere, or the shaman or holy man, named Buddha Lama, of the village in Nepal where I have close emotional ties. *Shaman? What means all this?*

And when I am alone there reviewing my assignment, and ordering up every last book online so they will be waiting for me when I am released from the Ranch, a storm of inconceivable proportion erupts, banging into the side of the building repeatedly; lighting the sky so brightly that even the double layer of room-darkening shades and draperies don't help; shutting off the power to the entire facility. Powerlessness!

It's a sign. Isn't it? Tell me it's a sign.

Chapter 4
Asserting My Powerlessness

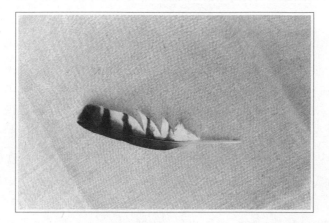

Give yourself to the Way
And you'll be at home on the Way.
Give yourself to power
And you'll be at home in power.
Give yourself to loss
And when you're lost you'll be at home.

—LAO TZU; URSULA K. LEGUIN
TRANSLATION

POWERLESSNESS. I HAVE BEEN SPENDING some mental energy and effort and money (on help) this late fall and early winter mouse-proofing, systematically plugging holes to keep them out, and once home from Camp Surrealistic Pillow I am back at it.

"The best way to get rid of snakes is to get rid of the mice," the wildlife control specialist from the local pest control place had decreed a month or two before, in high snake season, and so it was a one-two punch, really, that we resumed, trying to determine that neither rodents nor reptiles would spend the colder months tucked into the foundation, into the walls, or worse, in the dining room with me and the increasingly companionable Jack.

Hardware cloth and cement are stuffed in and slathered on the junctures where foundation meets ground outside. Inside, some kind of weatherproofing foam that dries a shiny dark gray, as if chunks of charcoal have been wedged between the rubble that is called the foundation of this lopsided little house of mine, where not just my life but also the literal underpinnings are regularly shifting. A ball placed in the back corner of the ground floor when I first bought the place would roll all the way into the living room, a distance of nearly thirty feet, as if possessed; now four house jacks and various lengths of lumber sistered to the aging log joists fight the forces for me.

Admittedly, life is a little bit upside down lately, and things here are never quite level, but can that be the explanation for the number of moles I keep catching in the many baited mousetraps in the attic? Moles, who have the ability to tunnel a couple of feet deep or farther and create extensive underground systems with their ambitious digging, never struck me as the third-story type, but there they are, or were. RIP.

The eastern mole is *Scalopus aquaticus.* In this animal's case that last word, or species, the modifier to the first word (the genus) is wildly misleading; yes, the eastern mole can swim, but it's not an aquatic species by nature; it's terrestrial. Perhaps mine are a new break in the species, *S. aquaticus* var. *atticus*?

But what the continuing activity upstairs tells me is that all that mouseproofing tomfoolery isn't working, and so I called the pest control guys for another visit on my guaranteed earlier work aimed at keeping critters and their predators the snakes out. Even afterward, I doubt anything has been solved and expect more moles and mice at any moment, but the stories the service rep came armed with were worth the price of the attempted exclusion. I don't get out much; the laughter was a real treat, since for this moment I was not laughing at me.

"I keep catching moles in the attic," the appointment began, and then, "You mean mice, right, lady?" And then, "No, I mean moles; paddle feet, tiny tails, very soft fur," and then, "Huh, well, that's a new one." *(What's a new one? A customer who can tell a mole from a mouse, or a mole in the attic, or both?)* And then knowing he was with an animal-savvy comrade, he let loose:

• With the story of the woman who called for help with the feral cat who got into her cellar and delivered a litter of kittens. But they weren't kittens; they were baby opossums (perhaps the fact that Mom was carrying them around in a pouch—the opossum being our only North American marsupial—should have been a tip-off, or maybe that rodentlike face with those tiny, rounded ears, and that scary, naked tail?).

• And then with the tale of the woman with the puppies just whelped in the shrubbery out front, the cute but unwanted stray puppies—you know, that family of coyotes.

• Or the saga of the man who'd bought a house formerly owned by a collector of snakeskins. Yes: dozens and dozens of long sheds from sizable reptiles, genus and species unknown—but impressive. "They kept the collection in the attic, hung over the rafters," the proud inheritor of said collection explained to the pest-control expert who'd come on a call about mice and just gotten to talking. And up to the top floor they went, through the hatch in the spare hall ceiling where the drop-down staircase barely fit past the bedpost—upstairs they went to see the precious stash.

Nothing a snake likes better than a warm place with something slightly coarse to rub against when it's time to cast off its old skin—like the rough-hewn timbers of those rafters in that uninsulated attic, perhaps? And where there are skins, there are...

And I was concerned about a few moles.

In the first years, I thought this business of mice was about the scariest thing involved in rural living, even of the weekend variety. Scratching in the walls; bodies (if you were lucky) in the traps to dispose of, smelly if it was the Friday-night patrol of the week's haul. And there was also the occasional live catch, meaning the choice of smashing the injured rodent with a broom (mercy killing?) or picking it up, trap and all, alive. And then there was Option 3.

I always knew what to do when I got a live one in a trap then: Call Herb (unless there was a man of the moment in residence to come to my rescue). Call Herb. If anyone knows my terrors as much as Dr. Goudard and now Jonathan, it is Herb, who has removed not just unfortunate mice on occasion but also helped me outsmart red squirrels in the upstairs bathroom and more skunks and raccoons and woodchucks underneath the house and outbuildings than I can even recall. I have no shame as big as my fears—just ask Flora, Herb's wife. "We know the real Margaret," she readily reminds me with her characteristic teasing smile, as if she will someday tell all.

What folly, the idea of anything-proofing, though, really. There is always another way in, a loophole or an actual hole, in everything; yes, of course I know that; I have been listening, Leonard Cohen, and have my share of Buddhist texts here littering the place, too, like you do, to tell me so. I have your lyric: *There is a crack in everything, that's how the light gets in.*

I know about cracks. In my favorite baby picture, a black-and-white image, I am standing in front of the garage of my childhood home in a pair of swimming trunks and thick rubber winter boots. I am carrying an umbrella, though the sun is glinting off my then-golden hair, which is in perfect braids. There is a wrinkle, however; the umbrella is kaput, more spokes than fabric, but the look on my face says the last bit is no matter to me whatsoever. Smile on.

This year, my second winter, I am determined that I will be ready for whatever comes with a higher caliber of equipment than in that long-ago and carefree moment. So I keep at it: making "if only" lists, list of things that (*if only I had them*) would make me safer, less afraid, a survivor. Lists for dealing with power outages, animals, ice, insanity. Armed and dangerous with things like these, I approach the battlefield of winter:

• Buy a portable generator in case of prolonged disaster, one I could manually fire up to keep things from freezing, if not completely comfortable. (The unlevel ground and the desire not to spoil the garden views makes installing an automatic propane backup device and its attendant tank a challenge.)

Check.

• When my sister asks what I want for Christmas, ask for camp lanterns with rechargeable batteries, so that I do not break my neck one of these nights when there is no power.

Check. (And: *Ho, ho, ho.*)

• Place weatherproof containers of traction grit and serious salt and appropriate scoops at all entrances to all buildings.

Check.

• Lay in a large stash of fifty-pound bags of both materials while ground is easy to navigate, to be used for refilling the containers above through the season.

Check.

• Replace the heavy older snow shovel with a lighter model.

Check.

• Put sandbags over axle of pickup truck to improve stability in case it's needed in winter, like if the regular car spins off the road into the woods, or worse.

Check.

• Change Saab tires over to snows.

Check.

• Buy two sets of Yaktrax cramponlike grippers for my shoes, one pair attached to shoes kept in the car and another on a pair in the mudroom.

Check.

• Stock both vehicles with an extra gallon of washer fluid (but only a brand rated to very low temperatures; not the usual stuff from the gas station); small shovels; scrapers; a broom; extra gloves; a flashlight.

Check.

• Get a battery-powered radio, preferably one specifically for weather reports.

Check.

• Keep BlackBerry and cell phone charged diligently for when landline and DSL go dead.

Check.

And then, of course:

• Keep an eye on the weather.

Check.

But that last one proves to be just another exercise in power-lessness, which I should have realized the very first time I read the language of meteorology:

Winter weather advisory. Winter weather warning. Icy mix. Ice storm. Freezing rain or drizzle. Mix of snow and sleet. Blowing / drifting snow advisory. Near-blizzard conditions.

And my favorite: Wintry mix.

What it boils down (freezes up?) to is this: activity limited; make no advance plans. This stuff in all its forms is treacherous, and you have to learn to sit good and still, like it or not. Winter's coming. Like this recent day—oh, ducky—that called for snow, sleet, ice, *and* wind, the superfecta of winter weather. Glad I've got me a ticket on that one.

Well, my Mama told me there'll be days like this.

Down the road, Herb is checking things off his own list, including (after the last leaf mulching) removing the mowing deck and putting the plow blade on his tractor, a tractor that is simply the older vintage of the same model as mine.

Are we ready?

SOON IT DAWNS ANOTHER GRAY DAY and is snowing lightly, and I am at the table: Margaret Roach Inc. corporate headquarters, I guess. Or at least it's the place where I seem to find myself a lot of these days of my deepening solitude, blogging or researching something or just IMing and Tweeting with the people who are now my circle of silent friends known not by their voices as much as their IM idioms and idiosyncracies: emoticons or not? Lol and btw and ftw and omfg, or everything spelled out? Known by their real name or something funny, like the one that my niece, then eleven, gave me on one account where she liked to video chat with Aunty: Aunty Monkey Butt. (Do you know, by the way, even a woman who lives alone gets to hear men holler during NFL games if she's on Twitter? I am virtually surrounded, and on Sundays they are rooting for every team in the nation, one after another, as my screen refreshes itself.)

Jack is at his usual post, transfixed before the glass door between the smaller of two mudrooms and the back porch, presumably watching Cat TV Network as things blow by his "screen" or a bird alights to quickly snatch a seed from the dormant, dry clematis vine that wraps the wooden columns. He has already completed his morning ritual, the practice he has taken on after breakfast each day: running up the steep old enclosed staircase that doubles as my file holder, the inside corner of each step devoted to a project or topic of paperwork, up all eleven steps and then the landing. He makes a sharp right and heads into the study at the top, navigating straight for a framed photo of my father's 1920-something college graduation portrait, which still sits on the floor at the far end of the room, leaning against the wall, never rehung (along with several other pictures) since my move-in date many months back. Up he runs to it and paws at the glass, at the sepia-toned face of my father, who will be dead for thirty years any day now, and then he heads back down to sit with me, today on top of a scattered heap of old love letters I have found upstairs and been reading through haphazardly. Ah, yes, now we are settled in: an insistent kneading of the paper pile with his front paws, a circle or two, and down.

The phone startles me; I can see from the caller ID readout

that it is Jay, the professional matchmaker I hired late last summer to try to add Mr. Right to the developing photograph of My New Life—and perhaps another set of love letters to the increasingly musty vintage pile. (*Who were some of these people?* I am wondering, looking at the odd lot of handwriting and postmarks. *Whose life was that?*) The only other real phone calls these last ten days or so in the countdown to the Christmas holidays have been the expected annual ones: people checking in simply because we haven't in some time.

Holidays bring that out in everyone: the yearly calls, catching up. Two ex-boyfriends have already logged their seasonal remarks; I am expecting the casualty count to hit four by the weekend, as it always does, and all the calls are tinged to some degree or other with the guilty or at least regretful "whatever happened to our friendship?" that is the watermark of connection diluted by time and lack of interaction.

But not this one: Jay is all about tomorrow, not the past, and he is also on a mission and wants to talk about the latest group of men he has sought out for me, part of a private search I upgraded to a few months later, a campaign that he has done for an additional fee in the thousands beyond the basic preposterous price of entry into his big, digital date book of bachelors, to try to locate men who live nearer by. The first few candidates all lived in the city or weekended in the Hamptons or Connecticut; *how would we ever see each other?* I kept saying, and from those out-loud wonderings came the upgrade to a private search. Money is no object, right? I am fully unemployed.

It's mid-December, and the rest of the world is winding down to a productivity standstill, while Jay is apparently rushing to match every last client he can before his upcoming television-taping-that's-maybe-a-dream-come-true experience, set to start shooting in Los Angeles the first week of January, engulfs him. In my behalf, Jay has been networking and advertising in my surrounding area since November; not the ideal time to do so, when everyone is increasingly holiday-minded, but there is the matter of the upcoming TV commitment that we must either rush to beat or decide to wait for its completion.

We rushed, apparently forgetting this: *You can't hurry love, / No, you just have to wait.* Sing it, Diana.

When the phone rings I am thinking *maybe we shouldn't have,* but the check's been cashed; the ads have been placed; the respondees prescreened by phone by Jay and company. Time for him to come up north and meet the standouts from the lot, of which there are ten, he says. He and a colleague are doing so day after tomorrow, he says, which besides being the weekend before Christmas is also predicted to be no ho-ho-ho or winter carnival, weatherwise. Good rural resident that I am, I have been watching the weather (*check*). "A storm is coming," I say. "A big storm, Jay."

"Some people are weatherwise, but most are otherwise," said Benjamin Franklin. Yup. Here we go proving that chilling maxim.

In fact, we already have a Winter Storm Watch (no mere Advisory) and from the looks of it on the Almighty NOAA's website, it will soon become a Winter Storm Warning, the strongest form of admonition. The National Oceanic and Atmospheric Administration is nothing if not full of friendly reminders, always slightly stern-sounding and sensible like Grandma's, and always for your own good. You know the type. Incredibly irritating, but often right.

Jay is not worried. He will call when they are leaving Philadephia, he says, to check for updates. And he does, and I (now in a Winter Storm Warning and doing my last steps in prestorm protocol here, like filling the buckets beside each toilet to flush them manually if the power and all else fails, and refilling my sand and salt bins) say, "Forget it, don't come," and he says, "It seems fine here," and then my part again: "That's five hours to the south, Jay," but my logic is lost.

And then there are the cell phone calls throughout the snowy day with progress reports: a nearly impassable New York State Thruway; some exits closed; very slow going; no visibility to be seen anywhere. He is risking his safety and that of his colleague to find me Mr. Right, and I am thinking that is crazy, completely crazy, but he keeps driving anyhow, my Road-Warrior-for-Hire.

The normal drama of a storm day—when it is already hard here to concentrate on anything but the weather—is heightened because I am living this one out in two places: on the road with Jay, and here. He probably doesn't even have real snow tires on that new BMW, but it's much too late to ask that question. (Lesson learned the hard way: "All-season" or "all-weather" tires mean all seasons or weather except for winter here. *Check.*)

I don't want a man with whom I am not even involved to perish in the name of my connubial connection. *No matter how much I shelled out, Jay, please stop driving*; this is just plain madness, life-threatening madness. Pull over and admit defeat. As I had warned (having read my Winter Storm Warning, *check*), the snow is falling as fast as two inches per hour, the kind of white-out conditions that even the plows don't tackle until it desists. I measure a foot on the ground.

All the while through the wild day and the one that follows (when Jay the Triumphant, Vanquisher of Blizzards, arrives in the general vicinity and starts interviewing the bachelors), whenever I can get past my terror for just a moment, I think, on the other hand, maybe this is it: *Maybe it's a sign. Maybe it's magic.* Perhaps I never found "him" because I never turned the volume up this high before, never sent a messenger out in my behalf against the forces to risk life and limb for the cause. *Yes! This will be the answer.* I try to prevent it, to stifle the madcap magical thought process that leads to *this is it*, but maybe, just maybe. *Maybe it is.* Will I start the New Year with the promise of a hot date?

At nearly four o'clock on New Year's Eve afternoon, the e-mail arrives: "Some of us are having a holiday dinner down at the T-I," it says, short for Taconic Wayside Inn, technically the only year-round, full-time business in town besides the post office. The little store at the former depot and a bike shop across from it mostly cater to seasonal park visitors, and open on a schedule as such. And then the e-mail asks this: "Join us?"

I write back that I am already (always?) wearing my pajamas, only halfheartedly deflecting the invitation, and not two minutes later comes this:

"PJs are just fine."

I cannot recall one New Year's Eve that I enjoyed; I like to stay home, and rarely have I seen midnight. But this invitation did not come laden with any of that "it's a big deal" energy that always ruins such holidays with its great expectations. It was just someone—a little bird, actually, since her name is Robin—being neighborly; it was already getting dark and there would be plenty more nighttime left to spend alone after supper, which was at six. And so I went.

Maybe fourteen of us, from teenagers to others well into their seventies, half their faces unknown to me, gathered at a long table filling the left-hand parlor of the unassuming old stagecoach inn; the right-hand parlor, just through the archway by the stairs, long ago became the town's one bar, the kind with beer-sign lights and a pool table and TV tuned to sports. I have rarely been inside this solitary eating and drinking establishment of our town, and not in ages, so no surprise, really, that even after more than twenty years owning my home here, I still do not know my neighbors, though they know me—the Martha lady, the lady with the big garden and the tours—the odd woman out. But now, at this extended table of my new extended family, I am the odd woman in. Happy New Year; happy new life?

Semifreddo Silence

I SMELL SMOKE AGAIN; why is someone burning brush on such a bitter day, and so early? But oh, yes, there's the explanation: Cracking the door a little wider than I had a moment before to assess what I'm up against in this morning's shoveling, I also pick up on the low whir of a diesel-tractor engine, a hum I know can only be Herb coming down the road to dig me out. The smoke is not from brush at all this time, but Herb's cigar. As Susan says in fairer months, on days when she is working with me in the garden, "You can always smell Herb coming." I must hurry.

This time twelve inches have fallen in total, but I already shoveled several rounds last night; that's how winter works here—you take it in stages or it is just too much to grapple with. Depending on the rate of snowfall, I shovel every hour or two or every half day, timing my duty to every few inches of snow, so that it is not too much for me to move, even if it's the wet and heavy variety. The most insidious storms do all their snowing while we sleep; *you snooze, you lose*, those devilish blasts seem to say, wagging a giant white finger. Clobbered.

Herb and I have practiced our snowplow pas de deux for decades, but never with so many encores in a season as since I am here full-time. It's the same routine we used when storms coincided with my days in residence all those years, storms I hoped would fall so late in the weekend and so heavy that I would not be able to return to the city, which I always called going "back," not "home," for reasons I understand more each passing day. Now that I am here to do the routine so many times in a week, I wonder how he managed solo; who played my part, and what the rhythm he'd composed, the one that I am now interrupting, had been like?

There is no real driveway here, at least not any longer. When I first came to the house, the drive went all the way up, ending right alongside the kitchen, so the passenger side of the parked car was perhaps just four feet from the building. A mark of my profound unconsciousness then is that I really never noticed, despite all the hours facing the stove—and the car—with every supper made, or pot of applesauce stirred, or Ball jar of pickles, jam, or plum tomatoes processed. Perhaps a dozen years into my stupor on the matter, a visiting gardening friend who was frying the eggs for our lunchtime egg sandwiches looked out the kitchen window and simply said: "Do you like looking at your car instead of at the garden, Margaret?"

Huh?

The local dozer guy came for an estimate the next day, and erased the old driveway not long afterward, layering on some top-soil and sowing grass seed, at first, which over time got dug up, chunk by tentative chunk, in favor of a walkway and then more beds and eventually a big stone skirt around the house, connecting walk to doorway. That driveway erasure was one of the best garden-design decisions ever made on this piece of land, and an expenditure I have never regretted, though in winters since it has meant that a delicate dance is required to find a place to put the snow down below, in the small, very unevenly pitched parking area that remains between the road and the little barn that not so long ago rose up on the footing of an older one that was crumbling.

The resulting tight spot means no plowing in the conventional way by pushing the accumulation of snow anywhere is possible; a front-mounted plow despite all its brute force is thus rendered impotent. Like one of those Olympic dives requiring expert calculation and grueling hours of practice, this plowing thing here now has a very high degree of difficulty: Only a small plow blade on the back of a nimble tractor with a trim turning radius can maneuver and push it bit by bit downhill, across the dirt road, into the adjacent woods of the parkland.

That is, unless the town plows have made a wall of snow and ice like a quarter-pipe ski-jump course across the way already—a barrier that when there are enough storms with repeat thaws and freezes will then remain a looming glacier till May. *Nowhere to put your snow? Sorry, lady. Did you say you were claustrophobic?* Bringing new meaning to the expression "feeling boxed in."

But yes, I must hurry; no time for that tea today, not yet. Herb is here, my best and most faithful dance partner. Quickly, quickly: a puff of my inhaler; an extra pair of pants over my pajamas; a bra beneath my nightshirt and a hooded sweatshirt and a jacket on top; glove liners and gloves; thicker socks; big boots with cramponlike metal springs (the Yaktrax) affixed to the bottoms for the way down and up again; a pocket stuffed with Kleenex and the car keys; the broom; the shaker-dispenser of ice melt; the best of the many imperfect snow shovels, the one whose orange plastic blade is shaped like a piece of storm-drain pipe cut in half, the one I can simply push on the downhill route to move aside some snow and get to where Herb is already beginning the entrée of this performance. *Phew.*

Oh, please, let the stuff be dry and light enough for simply pushing easily aside like that, instead of the snow that requires lifting and tossing, too. I must hurry, as much as one can hurry when the path is steep and the surface slick. With each step I hear a little voice saying *broken hip* inside my head, and so I walk deliberately in a forced gait of tiny, stiff-legged steps, forcing myself not to risk it. My entrée to this dance is not so graceful. Thankfully, we have no audience, save a few hardy birds.

My first act begins. The role I play while Herb (stubby cigar still stuck if not by now frozen to his lower lip) is already well along in his adagio, pushing the snow from the longest, four-blade-passes-wide leg of "driveway" into and across the road, looks like this: I sweep off the car; get it started and deice the windshields, making it ready for when it's my turn to really move. Once he has cleared that longest spit, I go: up and over the ridge of snow left in front of the tires from his last pass, out into the road, to wait somewhere, in any remaining open patch big enough to tuck into safely, depending on the severity of the storm—the defroster's fan adding its voice to the chorus, accompanying the duet of the engines.

For the next few minutes, then, we are each deep into our solo variations: one at a time, no longer onstage together, before we finally reunite for the coda. Herb, still puffing between blade strokes, makes his last pass and raises an arm to signal me, and up I come, on cue, hoping to gain sufficient speed from where I have been waiting downhill apiece to navigate the sharp left into my drive again, without fishtailing into the metal farm fence or worse, a tree.

Tada! Another performance of the driveway-plowing ballet behind us, Herb raises his arm once more, in the same small, formal wave of that first day of our meeting decades ago, and then is off, the cigar's scent and the whirring of the elder of two Kubota tractors in our connected lives fading gradually until all falls scentless and silent again here, muffled in white. We never said one word.

I AM SEEING A LOT OF HERB THIS WINTER, or at least we just keep dancing, our performance schedule dictated by the heavens as my entire life seems to be these days. Between these impromptu appointments, which seem to vaguely irritate the audience of woodpeckers that call the old, gnarly maple by the roadside parking area home, I am struggling to fill that schedule of mine. All these months later it still contains only a few items: *Make tea* (daily); *feed cat* (daily); *take out trash* (once weekly, at Wednesday dawn); *talk to Dr. Goudard* (twice monthly, on Tuesday evenings).

Do yoga tries to get on the calendar, but never makes it, a year now without its own permanent, ritual spot, despite repeat attempts.

I am telling time by the time and date stamp atop the NOAA map that I scan anxiously throughout each day, wondering what's heading for me. (Sadly, among its many layers of carefully calculated prognostications, NOAA does not offer services to foretell where I am headed, an estimated time of impact, nor the percentage chance of my ever getting there.)

I realize that I can also now tell time and the weather with my ears, at least a little, and at certain moments. Though the road is in the direction of the back of my chair (and head), I hear Herb's purple truck passing, heading toward town. It has become a game: I look up and yes—*correct, Margaret!*—it is just about eleven AM, time for him to travel the five miles to Hillsdale and the diner for daily coffee with his longtime cronies. On time, as ever; that's my clock named Herb. In forty-five minutes or so, he will make a pass in the other direction. Yup, there he goes. *Score!*

Methodical, predictable drive-bys of the town plow are like that, but move in reverse. Their first sweep comes from the northeast end of the road, driving on the far side parallel to my boundary, and it is only thirteen minutes before the return pass happens, this time with the giant blade hugging the edge of my land, nipping at it hungrily.

Icicles let go from the roofline, forming disturbing, loud punctuation points to an otherwise silent midday. It must not be anywhere close to as cold as yesterday, I calculate, if the giant stalactites are already being whittled down to the breaking point. The buildup outside the second-story bathroom window, near where the satellite dish is positioned to face the desired south and west, is so bad that no pulse has gotten through in more than a week; "Searching for Satellite Signal" is all my television screen has to say for itself. *No, you search for it; I am busy with my own investigations. Catch you later.* Perhaps one of us will have an illumination or make a connection sometime soon, emphasis on perhaps.

"My" nonstop station, the alternative-music public-radio channel WFUV from down in the Bronx, at Fordham University, has given way to Pablo Casals playing solo cello suites by Bach, the same two discs spinning again and again in the five-disc CD changer in the other room, the sound of the late master's solitary brilliance filling the house with *yes-you-can* energy. Not so long ago, I prided myself on keeping up with new music, something that always surprised the youngest people who worked for me. Now the voices would distract me, and so instead I listen to this one set of remastered vintage recordings of a man alone with his instrument, a session recorded around the year of my birth.

It is so quiet some winter days that I feel as if I have on the uncomfortable noise-reduction earmuffs that I wear when on the tractor, mowing or moving mulch in garden season. Besides Herb's predictable movements and the occasional crash of ice, the only sounds now are more subtle: one or another of various woodpeckers, from the pileated to the tiny downy, or the salt-induced glacial erosion I cause with my incessant maintenance of the walkway. *Snap, crackle, pop.* (Maybe I do this routine enough now that it qualifies for a spot on the schedule, in one of the vast blank spaces?) No woman wants to be an island, especially not one separated from the mainland by a bridge of solid ice, but despite my hyperdiligence bordering on paranoia and even

OCD, I come perilously close on many occasions. Even with my crampons strapped to my toughest rubber and neoprene farmer's boots, I don't feel safe.

I've fallen, even when I haven't fallen, and I can't get up—or out.

Can't or won't? I can hear Dr. Goudard now. *Nobody's going to fly in your window, Margaret.*

Actually, the signs are mixed on that score: Again we prove the good doctor wrong, and my vigil is rewarded regularly with reminders to just sit still. In they do fly; *na-na-na-na-na.*

As if on cue, a blue heron provides evidence to support my side of the case, flying overhead in an improbable move I don't expect in such cold times, particularly because I have no substantial body of open water here to offer him. I take it as an omen, and a reminder to just keep at it. *(Follow the signs!)* The heron is a symbol of self-reliance; his long legs can handle life's deep waters, into which he often puts just one, and he is a bird of land, too, and sky. Hello, my liminal friend. And there is more: This solitary hunter—as thin as I am—finds his way to sustenance alone.

When I am needed, of course, I can respond in an instant, without thinking, like when a tufted titmouse hits the western window, the best one in the house, that one with the views and the light. Apparently the strengthening sunshine of this midwinter day has confused the little gray bird with the distinctive crested head, and he flies into the window, if not actually in. *Shit.* I know that he won't last long immobilized in this weather. I rush out without my boots, and there he is: buried facedown in a drift, from which I scoop him out quickly and hold him gingerly but close to my body, sharing my warmth.

At this moment I am thinking of something it says in the teachings in one of those 127 woo-woo books out there in the other room: *When you are afraid, put your head in the lap of the Buddha.*

The titmouse's big black eyes, tiny bulging onyx beads, are moving all around; he is alive but he is so stunned at where he finds himself, and struggles to reset his jangled interior compass. *Come on, little one, come on: Get your balance back.* And then he rights himself in my palms, looks at me steadily for one unblinking second, and off he flies. My own interior gaze shifts from the Buddha to Burroughs, the Victorian-era New York State naturalist:

> The live bird is a fellow passenger; we are making the voyage together, and there is a sympathy between us that quickly leads to knowledge.

Between such moments of magic, truth be told, I feel headfirst in a snowbank, too; stuck, or at least *semifreddo*; never alone or lonely, but somewhat betwixt. There are other signs that reinforce the feeling, ones that remind me it's midwinter: Locust trees in the woods make cracking sounds like shotguns on the coldest days. The foundation heaves, leaving the back door rendered useless until the next insult, the one of mud season, eventually comes on. The cat is really upset; he doesn't grasp my offer of the porch window as exit-entry—one of three ground-floor windows in my direct gaze that I keep unfitted with screens so I can hope to see clearly, without any of the screening's shadowy light reduction. He wants his door. I want mine, too, the certain path across the frozen threshold that I am living on, but it is jammed.

Nearby, a closet door won't open, either; probably that was not a good place to hang the winter (read: needed it now) outerwear. But I only have two miniature closets here, so what really was the choice? Seems odd to keep the coats up in my bedroom; seems odder to realize I may be without use of them until April, maybe May. Old foundations have minds of their own when they get together with serious frost, behaving as if there is no today. (Poor planning; put *better coat storage solution* on next year's prewinter prep list. *Check.*)

When this ground-floor heaving shows itself, I know I should look to see if any stones in the basement walls have dislodged, meaning someone big could get in. But that would mean going on mouse patrol, and I am not in the mood for dead bodies with tails right now—mice who have perhaps met their end in one of the many peanut-butter-filled traps placed down there year-round.

Instead I cross to the freezer to take out a cube or two of the summer's homemade pesto. Later, defrosted and spread on crackers, it will be a welcome green blast of summer on the tongue. And I look for more bright bits, like the fact that despite its other downsides, this is the perfect nonchemical moth-control weather. Suspect any in your woolens? Put them outside for several days below eighteen degrees, like right about now. I wonder what the big Buddha thinks when I hang my suit jackets and other old career gear from the porch rafter, a straight shot from his vantage point on things? No matter, really, since his eyes remain closed.

The odd lot of clothing moving in the breeze the next few days is my only local color, animated scarecrows all in a line. Otherwise, I am not seeing much of anybody. I haven't been anywhere since a couple of storms ago, when Jonathan told me he was coming east again, this trip with two well-known author colleagues, and I went to talk with him a second time—and meet them both. I brought home three more books covered in the promise of answers (at last count, the total in the other room is in the 130s), but frankly I cannot even read them, as far inward as I seem to have turned. I can't even really sort any of what they all talked about yet, though I took notes, which include some whopping Freudian slips like this:

"It's silly to *live* in your own fantasy," I wrote in my urgent scrawl, the familiar penmanship used during lectures that I am excited by. But here's the thing: Jonathan had paraphrased John-Roger, founder of the Church of the Movement of Spiritual Inner Awareness, by really saying this: "It's silly to *lose* in your own fantasy."

And on another page, there's this real doozie: "my Martha," I scribbled, when what would complete the sentence was really "my mantra." With my own hand, I swear, I wrote just that. And it was not the only time.

Apparently I am having some entitlement issues.

"Tuesday," I say out loud to the sleeping cat, out of nowhere, as I am inclined to do fairly regularly, no matter the actual day of the week. "Tuesday, Jackie." And then it strikes me: September 11, the day Jack came to me, was a Tuesday. All these shreds of meaningful meaninglessness are bubbling up and out, suddenly in the grasp of semiconsciousness—*is that a sign?* My gaze, so long fixed or frozen on just making do while doing for others, is thawing, and like the closet door I expect it will have a wider range of movement soon. But not all at once, and not right now, please. Right now, all signs point to a glass of wine.

★   ★   ★

MORE THAN OTHER MALE STRAYS I HAVE LIVED WITH, Jack knows the mother of all lessons: Don't shit where you eat. He is a faithful cat, promises nothing he will not deliver, and is pretty straightforward about his limitations. He would never tell you he will not chase another bird. There will be others; you must lead him not into temptation with daytime liberty.

Though I am perhaps by this second winter-approaching-second-spring still not a cat person, exactly, I acknowledge that he has grown on me, and apparently the same is true in reverse. I do not realize how much until the incessant snow begins to thaw a bit at a time, uncovering what's beneath. As each layer vanishes it is clear that Jack has been systematically and with great care using the spot right outside the best window (the window where I sit every day, all day, as he well knows) as his personal toilet. One after another, with the easing weather, his offerings surface.

After the ice age we have just been through, they look like coprolites, the fossilized poop of archaeological discoveries and revelations, but in fact they are simply cat shit.

For you, Mommy. And another. All for you. Frozen in time, layers and layers of old shit.

While once he would attack at the very hint of a brushing, he seems to understand that it is the price of admission to Margaret's House of Hairlessness, and stops in the passageway between the door and his food bowl farther inside for the requisite ritual. We are up to many brushings a day as winter draws on, his extraheavy coat beginning to loosen a bit gradually with the fewer frigid days.

What I cannot blame him for happens next, on the last day of February, in an unseasonable warm spell that feels more like the last of March or even April. It is a seductive day, but not one to be trusted—why can I not learn the difference? The bullfrogs know something's up, meteorologically, and start to bob to the surface and even lumber out from beneath the thick but shrinking slab of ice that covers their pool. The biggest one, my favorite from last season and probably four years of age by now so an old friend, served as the unit's advance guard, emerging to sit a minute and survey the scene topside. Then Frog on Ice quickly got cold feet and headed back beneath the melting surface. Later, gator.

I sat out there awhile yesterday and photographed him, as I do every plant and animal I can get into my viewfinder, glad to have a subject showing itself aboveground so early. I'm not alone anymore! And then, a day later—this morning—I went to say hello again. Apparently the melting snow had also stirred the skunks, whose winter burrows are somewhere beneath it, or maybe a raccoon, and one hungry mammal or another had awakened ravenous and caught my senior frogboy and eviscerated him, leaving me the partly eaten carcass to consider on the stones beside the pool.

Listen to the signs? Well, then I have a lot of shit and dead bodies to consider here as my consciousness begins to thaw.

UNPLANNED, OR PERHAPS MADE TO HAPPEN in unconscious preparation years ago, the big Indonesian bust of Buddha out back is on a direct axis from my chair and eye-to-eye level when I am seated at the dining table, some forty feet away. So when I am looking inward while staring outward, as I am so often these melting-freezing-melting days, he is having fun with me. No wonder the big guy always smiles.

Buddha and the snow (*Remember, nothing lasts!*) do their own kind of dance, a game of hide-and-seek, or maybe of masterful illusion. Some mornings after a snowfall or when the wind blows things around, only the bump of his *ushnisha* (all loaded with that infinite, enviable wisdom) pokes out from the covering of white, and then the cloak recedes a moment later with a puff of wind or a few minutes of sunshine, and there he is again, facing me, though with eyes closed, deep in his own meditation, his inward-facing gaze.

Now you see him, now you don't; his cunning shell game. A little bit of Buddha, or not; being and nothingness. And I hear that saying again, the one that won't shake loose from my mind's ear lately:

When you are afraid—as I have undoubtedly scrawled with a pencil on some endpaper in one of those insistent books in the living room; if only I could find the one—*put your head in the lap of the Buddha.* Slogans, I've got, *Get your slogans here.* But my Buddha is a trickster, not to mention a mere bust without a lap anymore, and he's inclined to duck behind a drift of ephemera without notice, whenever the breeze kicks up.

In March, there is always much buffeting to be endured. This year, more so.

The stretch of woodsy jungle across from the driveway so wants cleaning out of all those vines and half-dead trees. I can see this ugly reality again as the glacial ridge that the town snowplows left behind begins to recede with sunnier days, but these acres are oddly absent of the pulsing of Herb's chain saw. We had applied for and received a permit to do the needed thinning on that overgrown bit of state land, and Herb was at it in his dogged fashion and then he was gone; something about having hurt his back, and pain down one leg. The man of few words but much action is watching football games on the living room couch down the road a little more than usual, is all, and though I know it goes against Herb's grain in the deepest way to leave anything half finished, the woods can wait another week or two or three.

The chain saw irritates me, anyway, its noise a bitter pill that must be swallowed to get the desired results. It's good burning weather, though, with the remaining snow cover to prevent any spread of fire, cover that presumably will soon melt. Too bad we aren't able to proceed with the cleanup, but no; not meant to be, and anyhow, Buddha and I are having a staring contest, sitting together in quiet meditation, each on our immovable spots as if awaiting awakening. Om, not *vroom*. Let it go.

L'Hermitage. Maybe that is what I should have named this place (though the idea of naming one's house or garden always struck me as way too fancy for either the tiny wooden building or for me). But it is quiet here right now; it seems that I have really dropped out, and in the process also dropped in, way in, to my own interior landscape.

This is by no means my first solitude or dropping out, and so most of the time, as it deepens and grows quieter despite the melting freeze outside, I know it is not a cause for worry. *Been here, done this.* I am the older sister of a girl who is more like our mother than I would ever be—all outgoing and athletic those two—so I have played alone a lot, entertained myself, from a very young age. The outsider.

As I have said, Mommy tossed my Barbies and my precious

trolls when I moved out for college, from which I would quickly drop out—there's that phrase again—only to try another school and quit that one, too, a repeat offender in my early attempts at escape and at "finding myself," as we called it then. (Enrollment was eroded by ennui: I was rebellious, and also sad about my parents' messy marriage, and real-life newspaper experience was so much more thrilling than the theoretics of the classroom.) Even now, though, I can still feel what it was to be among those not-quite-human dolls in the entire village that I built on the floor of the basement playroom, with its big slate pool table and the floor of cold-to-the-touch, speckled beige linoleum squares. It was always cool and dark down there, even in the humidity and heat of high summer, when sister Marion and Mommy (read: not doll people) were probably up at the club, playing tennis then swimming vigorous laps, or perhaps out sailing (another item for my lifetime fear list, come to think of it; terra firma for me, please—don't cast me off upon any waves, at least not watery ones, I beg of you).

A landscaper of sorts, even then, was I; a builder of secret little worlds to live happily ever after in, at least if you were a troll. I brought in rocks and sticks from outdoors and fashioned roads between the school and the houses and yes, trees, always in the trees have I lived, even in my symbolic hamlet founded upon subterranean floor tiles. Happy ever after, me and those trolls, had they not perished at Mommy's hand. Funny to realize now how froglike their eyes were, and also their fixed, ultrawide grins; the faces of things to come. *Ribbit.*

Later, in my very own room two floors above, I was a young teen who would have preferred to skip most everything: the boys in junior high and their relentless teasing; phys ed classes and team sports; school dances and class trips; church on Sundays—all of it, strangely, except Girl Scouts, which I participated in until near adulthood. I lived a good deal inside my head, even then, I guess—and I also really liked s'mores. That's the only combined explanation I can offer, at least in short form, for the idiosyncratic behavior of a rebel girl in uniform. Dr. Goudard would know the long form; if you run into him in a line of Buddhists somewhere, do be sure to ask.

As much time as I have always spent alone, not necessarily doing what was on the developmental schedule or going where the in crowd goes, sometimes nowadays it's jarring when I look at the online weather map—my one constant guide—and realize it's Thursday again and I haven't even collected the mail since Saturday (or was that Friday? So hard to tell). I haven't even slid the big metal driveway gates open once, haven't put on any makeup in days—and that last bit's the closest I have come to shedding any skin so far in this adventure, I fear—going without a coat of some foundation said to defy age and other good stuff. To hell with all the trappings, nobody but Buddha's watching, anyway, and he's got his big old eyes wide shut.

I am like a broody hen, or some other devoted female bird; I have sat down and simply will not risk the successful hatching of what's next by daring to get up, at least not just yet. The fierce, ever-present tree swallow who dive-bombed my face all spring and summer last year, protecting what must have been back-to-back broods, got out more than I do. I felt vindicated to read in the science headlines lately that my friends the birds know a good nest—and stick with it—when they find it. The oldest continually used nest, with 2,500 years of service to generations of gyrfalcons, has just been discovered in Greenland.

Yes, I know how it sounds, and even I am occasionally momentarily alarmed or at least startled at where I find myself without any desire to get up, but it quickly passes; I am not really alone—*am I?* I just know I fit into some bigger picture.

When I start to think, *uh-oh, uh-oh, out on a limb,* I have tactics to apply, countermeasures to deploy, quotes and sayings and lines of songs to say, and sing. They provide the magical-thinking form of proof that I am not the first, nor the only, to just go sit somewhere when life moved past simple answers; when rote stopped working as a routine. I have reassuring tidbits like an interview I read with Leonard Cohen, when he was asked about his time in the Zen monastery, and specifically about "dropping out" (poor choice of words on the interviewer's part, apparently):

This is the very contrary of dropping out. Most people can't wait to get home to their house or apartment and shut that door and turn on the TV. To me, that's dropping out.

I am not tetherless, nor completely silent. Honoring my promise to stay in touch, to stay connected and have at least the one witness beyond Jack and the stone statue, I offer my confession to Dr. Goudard one alternate Tuesday evening. Forgive me, Doctor, for I am spinning:

I awaken a lot at three o'clock these neither-night-nor-mornings, restless; my sleep habits are changing. I don't go out, and though I shower and wash my hair each day, I could not claim to actually otherwise be ready for prime time in the grooming sense. (My old friends in the designer boutiques at the 50th Street office wouldn't know me.) I've lost my yoga practice somewhere. I don't even get out of the chair long enough most days to collect the mail. I talk to myself, and then I reply. I drink alone (to solve that I would have to simply not drink, I guess). Hmmmm...

"You could well be describing someone who is depressed," the Big Cheese says in his even, considered voice, and then, just as my heart starts to race, he quickly adds, "but I don't think so."

I don't think so, either—not this Margaret, not the one who collects songs containing the word *hallelujah* or any of its world-wide variants and turns them into mixes, one following another, hours of hallelujahs from world beat to high church to pure pop. Not me. I think I am just still slightly in shock, the washer drum within me still wanting to agitate but not sure just why, or whether to bother; my inner troublemaker wondering why we aren't *doing something*. I keep trying to tell it that we are (which perhaps can serve as at least partial explanation of why I talk to myself?).

I think that I am settling in, and that the awareness of that is causing a little rattling way inside: In memorium, RIP Margaret Roach, EVP; thirty-two-year career girl, onetime success, age fifty-three when last seen or heard from. I am not surprised that this is where I find myself, really—single and in near silence, staring out a window. But what's the next step? Even if this is not depression, is this okay, is it the next logical step from where I was? Why does *Who am I if I am not mroach@marthastewart dot com any longer?* keep haunting me; if I am neither working nor in a personal partnership, in service to some master or another, *who am I?*

One obvious answer is rural-resident-in-the-rough (very rough).

"You know you've really moved to the country when you have your first local haircut," my friend Bob, five years ahead in age and rural-living tenure, tells me with a twisted smile I can visualize even though he is across the county, and a phone line. Kute Kutz salon, here I come? I think not. I must retain at least this shred of dignity, I must.

Bob enjoyed big success in his career, too, and then he left, and so when I am mystified at the nonstate of my affairs or just want to express some dark humor about my latest outfit (*Did I actually go out in that combination of garments? Did I really buy those more-than-sensible shoes? Did I sleep in my clothes yet again?*), it is Bob who gets to listen. He is a touchstone these quiet months, softening the sense of hollow where Herb and his different kind of leveling effect has gone missing, and I am relieved when he says he fell asleep on the couch at nine himself last night (yes, fully dressed in his own daytime-into-nighttime clothes that look strangely like mine), and that the milk went bad because it's only him to drink it, and that no, he hasn't opened the mail in days, either, and isn't sure when he will get to it quite yet.

Winter in the country can do it to the toughest souls.

THE PAINFUL SILENCE, THE RESOUNDING ABSENCE of Herb's midmorning diner run and the chain saw and the weekly chats, is no longer broken by the crashing of icicles from eaves to earth, but will be any minute now by the spring peepers, the little chorus frogs with voices big enough to fill the nighttimes, at least. *Is that them?*

Or maybe that last sound was something else; it is still way too early for the gray tree frog, but then what is it? I need to really listen, and to think. *Concentrate.* It is daylight, so it's probably not the peepers, and after all, it's still the very last bit of March. But who, then? If it quacks like a duck, I will learn today, it's not necessarily a duck: It's sometimes a wood frog, the earliest of the frogs to go out looking to get himself some, a hunk of burning frog.

"You just stay right here," I say to the unfamiliar amphibian who's sitting happily on the lawn about twenty-five feet to the west of the house, where I have gone out with careful listening—and with planting some early lettuce seed—in mind. But there, right by my foot, is this brick-colored frog, perhaps two and a half inches long, a frog I do not know. *Hello, handsome—* whomever you are.

"Wait," I say (yes, out loud) to this unfamiliar face, "I want to get my camera."

Apparently he speaks English and I must seem nice enough, for he is there when I return. If I gave this frogboy my phone number, he is the kind who would call. And then we sit for twenty minutes together, less than a foot apart, in the sunshine that on any March day seems so miraculous, so hopeful. There is actual warmth in this light; perhaps progress toward a gentler season? The wood frog (as I will be able to identify him once I go back inside with all those newly captured pixels and look at the guidebooks) sits completely still in the way that frogs do—in the way that I do most of my days, too, now. I know he thinks I cannot see him because of the cloak of stillness; I know he thinks that he has not given himself away with any false moves. Unseen, hidden, he feels safe.

As I am lying on the ground and capturing him through the lens, pulling him into even closer focus, a black shadow crosses the frame, a shadow big enough to change the meter reading substantially. *What?* A second later, my field of vision goes bright again. I rest the camera on the unmown, faded turf—last season's grass since it has not started growing again yet; the grass that lived like a shut-in through the winter under ice, in the months when the house and my life seemed to be built on glass and not soil at all. And then I look up.

A bald eagle is watching me watch the frog, circling overhead.

Today an eagle is flying above me and it is bright and the sun is actually warm on my scalp and I am now friends with a rusty-colored frog who's wearing a dramatic black mask across his face—all of this is true, but I am still not sure what I am doing here. I am positively surrounded by guides, ones who speak and others who are merely symbol laden and don't, and I know they are trying to tell me something—and I also know I am in the right place, yes, that much is certain—but I am still not able to really grok what it is I am to do, big-picture. I can see my guides, at least, if not entirely hear or understand them. *(Can't or won't, Margaret?)* And I haven't stepped on or slept with any toxic snakes lately. Progress?

Maybe, but for now I must admit that I remain in the place Jonathan admonished me about months ago: still connecting to the science of nature, but not its metaphysical dimension, keeping at bay any attributes of mine that could figure into the story around me. In my defense, I must tell Jonathan that even John Burroughs didn't get all transcendental (despite living in the era of that movement), and remained a lover of the very fact of nature throughout his many days.

So yes, I am thinking (emphasis on think, not feel) as I read these herpetology books that nobody else I know has ever read, nor will. This frog is the only reptile or amphibian found north of the Arctic Circle; if its eggs are laid in water that subsequently freezes, no matter—they can survive frozen in time (which is why this masked guy is cruising the vicinity so early; his spawn are tough, and he knows it). Once hatched and metamorphosed into a frog, the wood frog hibernates each winter with up to 45 percent of its body actually turning to ice and its breathing, blood flow, and heartbeat stopped; the master of cryogenics. It makes me think of all those articles I used to read about insects and their diapause strategies: Some creatures can withstand anything, seemingly anything, and then spring to life again.

I'll be back.

I've been compelled by the subject of diapause for more than a decade, for instance, though at this very moment I do not even know where I first came across the word. Call it a consequence of having lived more than half a century with the name Roach, or of my long and intimate professional relationship to gardening and its attendant bugs. Suffice it to say, diapause found its way into my consciousness and has caught my increasing attention.

Women my age are more inclined to talk of menopause; for me the soundalike transition of diapause holds far deeper fascination. (There was nothing even vaguely remarkable about my own menopause, except that it began—yup—exactly when I changed my life and moved to the country. Out with the old; a clean sweep of my past, even hormonally.) The bug stuff is much more exciting to the solitary resident Roach here.

Diapause, explained most simply by entomologists, "is a suspension of development that can occur at the embryonic, larval, pupal, or adult stage, depending on the species." Mediated by neurohormones, this "dynamic state of low activity" usually occurs "in response to environmental stimuli that precede unfavorable conditions."

Read: Before the going gets desperate, the desperate get going. They shut down, getting very, very still, in order to survive. Sometimes for years.

Just as I was finding the path out of harm's way, another nature symbol signaled: A proposed update to the diapause theory was published, as if to call out to me.

Attention! Along with the reminder often comes a koan: a bit of wisdom you may not "get" right away, better understood through intuition than rational thought. But in this case my teachers were not wearing saffron robes. In August 2008, researchers at the University of Amsterdam published a study of female adult spider mites who, sensing predation from a literal scent in the air, induce diapause, "allowing them to move into an area where they are free of enemies, yet forced to survive without food."

I think I am there, I told myself as soon as I got to the house and my seat at the dining table, exhaling at the fact of finally being out of earshot of any predatory forces—the sirens of greed, the clinging to esteem, competitiveness, and the drive for pleasing others—that would have devoured me had I stayed a moment longer.

But I also knew even then that this retreat into stillness, this latest diapause of mine (yes, there have been others), was just a step, and that there were awakenings ahead.

God help me.

But I am quickly brought back to here and now from such

thinking, thinking because, again, the choir strengthens; today an orangey frog, tomorrow who will join in sounding the alert?

Wait—was that just a Greek chorus, coming in on cue? Ah, no, it is just the large group of local women who walk each day—the Walkers, as they are called by various people here—passing my point on the road, their voices swelling as if in some planned unison with some urgent message. One must really pay the very strictest attention to all life's goings-on; there could be clues, and messengers come in many guises.

They are among more voices that are arriving each day, each calling insistently with its own timbre, because apparently we have not yet reached a collective intensity that can get through to me. I can hear Burroughs all the while, urging us to have beginner's mind (he was writing about birding, not Buddhism): *The sensations of the first day are what we want....*

How loud will they have to turn it up, though, I wonder some days—and will my recognition kick in first, or will all this noise here in the deafening silence shatter my "inner" eardrum, the one they're banging on, the one I'm banging on, too; the one with the slightly deadened response, because (like the guy who works the jackhammer or chain saw too long) I so overdid it? Oh, listen, there's another now:

The bluebird males are back, and I think that is one up on the hill, at the oldest of the wooden nesting boxes, doing what male bluebirds do: the fake out. Scientists are kinder, and call it a "nest demonstration display," but it's a bait-and-switch; *be not fooled, sister.*

Yes, that's what this otherwise beautiful bird is doing, I am certain of it, walking into better position to watch. The male eastern bluebird's nest demonstration display (*ahem!*) goes like this: He brings bits of nest material to the hole, goes in and out, then waves his wings while perched above the box. *Honey, I bought us the nicest house*, he seems to say, *and some things to help us decorate. Please, honey, be mine.*

What a guy. Oh, except for this: That is pretty much Mr. Handsome's contribution to nest building, this bit of on-the-fly fakery with a twig in his beak, this stuff strutting, this PR job. Only the female eastern bluebird builds the nest and incubates the eggs. He's a big fat liar, and he (like that wood frog with his mask on, dare we ask what that's about?) is in the mood for some unencumbered sex.

I suppose all this—quacking frogs, scalawag birds—was going on the twenty-two years I was not here, and throughout time before that, but it feels like a series of firsts. *If a tree falls in the forest and nobody's listening,* and all that. Or John Lennon's fatherly admonition to the darling boy Sean: *Life is what happens to you while you're busy making other plans.*

But I have the oddest sensation, as if I'm standing at (or perhaps have actually become, deranged as that will sound) the center of the universe. Somehow, it's as if it was all ordered up for my entertainment: a command performance, a premiere. Invented for me: the wood frog; the nest demonstration display; the icicles that know they do not have forever in this strengthening light—*hurry before you're nothingness!* Even the wood thrush (*Hylocichla mustelina*), who capitalizes on their dripping onto the lower shed roof of the mudroom to enjoy a drink, its beak upturned, its awareness of the source of nectar that could let go and crush it—*now, now, now, now, now* (drip, drip, drip, drip, drip)—apparently nonexistent. We are all at risk with every action, or inaction. I am watching the play from my dress circle box seat, in my own theater, and in every scene one daring actor or another is melting, uncovering themselves, and maybe even waking up.

Eliot was exactly right; April is no friend. The season that is slipping by, even after all its icy tenacity, will soon sound kind. *Winter kept us warm, covering / Earth in forgetful snow.*

It is Friday, April 3, 2009. I am in the usual spot, seated facing the Lord Buddha, waiting for an e-mail or call from Herb's family to tell me how the surgery goes. *Surgery.*

The word takes me right back to a summer ago, when Marion—my baby sister, my only blood relative, as essentially we have been orphans since our twenties, children of two long-dead only children—needed surgery, the first time either one of us faced a major operation. I spent the weeks leading up to it intermittently crying and panicking, certain that she would die, consumed by nightmare tales of my own making that in no way related to her actual condition or diagnosis. *Surgery.*

Last Saturday, Herb pulled into the driveway not to chat, but to tell me something, to tell me that the laying low hadn't helped and that he needed surgery to remove a loose bit of bone alongside his spine. No big deal, he says, Herb-like. "I told them I can't be sidelined very long," he recounts, as if he is giving the orders. "I have to clean up the yard and get the garden ready for my potatoes." His vestigial New England accent lingers even now, in the "potatoes" and "yard," even after almost fifty years on this New York State dirt road.

Why haven't they called? It should be done by now. I remember sitting with Marion's husband in the surgical waiting room, until more than twice the estimated time for the procedure had elapsed, each of us pretending to the other that it was all just fine, but increasingly nonbelieving. *Make them call with the news.*

And so while I watch and listen for the Herb update, I am doing what I do a lot of the time at the lopsided wooden table whose joints need gluing and clamping yet again: I am blogging. Writing about gardening for my funny little garden blog named for a book I wrote years before, *A Way to Garden.* As in just one way, my way, not *the* way, necessarily. *(Note to self: need to write companion volume called* A Way to Live, *and urgently, and then please buy yourself a copy.)* I am collecting links from the existing site for some new feature sections I am building for the imminent spring, for the start of my second year on the Internet. *Hello, this is Margaret Roach Inc., can we help you?* (Can we even help ourselves?)

Search, click, highlight URL, command-C, highlight text to be linked, click "insert-edit link," command-V, click "insert link," voilà. And again. And again. And then, not again: The site is gone. What? Between the last round of this mind-numbing exercise of collecting and adding in old links to new pages, in the fraction of a minute it takes per round because I do this all the time and have turned into a robot, as Buddha is my witness, the site has vanished. Google dot com is there; Amazon dot com is there; my other blog is there, but...

Um, hello, hosting company? This is Margaret of A Way to Garden dot com and, um, my site seems to have vanished. Damsel in distress; not a role I love. I so hate sounding pathetic. There is no Rubbermaid antiskid mat large enough to prevent the dangerous slide I have just unknowingly taken. And as I am waiting for "Hi, this is Hank, how can we help you?" to help me, I am "saying" by simultaneous IMs to Brad, my own contract-freelance tech-support person: *Garden blog just disappeared; WTF?*

On the day that I experience my first malicious website hack, on the day that someone unknown and insidious is ripping into the precious strings of code that are my only contact of any substance with the outside world, my only remaining public voice albeit a tiny one as compared to the one I was part of for so many years before, the one I cast away, I am waiting to hear how dear Herb is doing under the knife. I call to check. The surgery has gone into double overtime; there are complications.

What? The small pieces that I have managed to fit together, that I count on for what little structure I do enjoy, feel way too fluid and tentative suddenly. Who am I if I am not (at least) Margaret of the tiny hand-built world of A Way to Garden dot com? Who am I if I am not (unthinkable, unthinkable) Herb's ex-flatlander neighbor? *Who am I?*

Oh, and here comes the answer, as if on cue: a violent electrical storm, with booming, rolling thunder, in case I wasn't listening. Powering down; save the computers, at least, if not my website or my sanity.

Attention, attention!

April is the cruellest month, with double *l*'s as Eliot intended, and we are barely three days in.

The abrasive, ripping noises of a chain saw would sound good right now. My personal silent spring is getting under way early, and even I, a deliberate cultivator lately of quiet and contemplation, cannot bear to listen to all its vastness, to this vacuum of longing.

The rest of the month (and the next and even into June, though I thankfully do not know it will go on so long then on this already very bad first day) will be spent in additional attempted procedures, each one meant to finally be the one that will fix (my site, Herb's health—take your choice; fill in the blank). Together we who have been felled—neighbors and old friends—must be rehabilitated, painfully and slowly, but not without being felled time and time again, once more with feeling, made powerless over and over, our noses and our pride and our pioneer souls rubbed in our helplessness as if we deserve such punishment. One step forward, and back to zero. Repeat.

Now you see us, now you don't.

Incoming (and Outgone)

EXCRUCIATINGLY, BUT FINALLY, IT TURNS INTO MAY. Wild turkeys are gobbling madly in the distance, up at the edge where the field meets the woods, where acorns and beechnuts overlooked or not yet surrendered before the snow flew combine with newly hatched insects and greening grasses, among other delicacies, for an omnivore's buffet. The sound, a ridiculous descending *gobble-gobble-gobble*, always makes me laugh; what a silly voice they have, those big old birds. It is quite a different matter, more startling than amusing, though, when a flock tries to take off and fly if spooked, their short, rounded wings having to raise as much as sixteen pounds of body (in the case of an adult tom) off the ground pronto.

Deafening.

It is also stranger than truth that these giant lumps carried on long legs with seemingly mismatched thin necks are the sprinters of the bird world: able to fly very short distances at very high speed (more than eighty-eight kilometers per hour). They possess the capability of an F-35 screeching off the flight deck, but with the dumpy body of a dirigible.

Fortunately the gobblers are not inclined to head in my direction at that velocity, but lately *Meleagris gallopavo* is about the only species that isn't. Sexed-up birds are slamming into windows daily these May days, as if insistent that I *let them in now*.

Nobody's going to fly into the window, Margaret. Oh, really?

I keep expecting more lightning, like last year in that most violent of springtimes, but there is almost no rain this month and therefore no fireworks; just these crashes—*incoming!*—and the rescue missions that follow. Primitive mankind thought that birds brought the thunder and the rain, but so far all I have this month is birds.

A male rose-breasted grosbeak, *Pheucticus ludovicianus*, his clean white chest emblazoned with a vibrant splash of red, hit a week ago, and I rushed to sit beside him on the fieldstones of the patio to the west of me, outside the window with the best light and view.

It had been an ovenbird, *Seiurus aurocapillus*, a few days prior, a gentle little thrush look-alike of a warbler with a big, wide-eyed stare and slender beak. He took more than twenty minutes to gradually go from lying down to standing to hopping and then flying off, all the while right beside me.

"You will be all right, just take your time," I told each of them in his terrifying turn. "We'll just sit here together until you are feeling ready to get on your way again, I promise." I have become the bird whisperer; it is a job I am good at, telling the fallen or disoriented or downright lost and left for dead to rise above their current circumstance and fly once more. Stand on your own two feet—funny, isn't it, that this creature of the heavens is one of very few but man that isn't four-legged? Most days this bird whispering is the only urgent task I face at all, she who once put out fires for a living.

And then another afternoon it was that noise again—a crashing at the back-porch window—and the most astonishing bird of all drops: the male scarlet tanager, *Piranga olivacea*. When I get out there not ten seconds later, he is lying on his side and looks to be a goner, all misshapen, like something major has been broken. *I know, you beautiful boy*; how hard to be incapable of flight, to have one's essential trait and bearings suddenly out of reach.

"No you're not, no you're not," I am saying to the reddest bird of all, his color as surprising as when I've come upon the cardinal flower, *Lobelia cardinalis*, in the shade of the woods here. The bird is now doing a good impersonation of the death throes; *yes, bird, I know, angels have wings, but let's not go there*. I am leaning my back against the warm siding under the porch overhang; the sunshine that glinted and confused the bird, creating a mirror effect on the panes, has also made it feel like July out here. "You can do it." He is so limp, even I am not certain, but it is what I want people to say to me on the bad days, when I grow afraid, and what I tell myself. Birds of a feather; do unto others.

Of course, these hideous mishaps are also fascinating. These are all birds I can identify even from quite a distance, their shapes and habits and flight patterns familiar to me. But even with that advanced-amateur knowledge I am unprepared for what their colors and patterns look like close-up, and at the intricate layering of their distinct types of feathers—what a gross generalization that word proves to be. *Feather* could mean remiges, rectrices, coverts, afterfeathers, bristles, each of those with further subcategories and each with a distinct purpose. Respectively, they are for flight; stability and control; streamlining and insulation;

extra warmth; or (like the whiskers of a cat) for some tactile experience and perhaps protecting the eyes when consuming certain prey. There are special ever-so-tiny feathers just for funneling sound into a bird's ear, the auriculars or cheeks, and I can see them now in a way I am not normally aware of. *Can you hear me, bird? Funnel this bulletin alert in there, now: You must get up.*

Yes, bird by bird, we are going to make it. We are. Liftoff, liftoff, and liftoff then again. I had thought last year, during my first spring here, that I might move forward frog by frog, but someone changed the script.

MINE IS A STILL LIFE WITH WOODPECKER. A yellow-bellied sapsucker (*Sphyrapicus varius*) is drumming incessantly somewhere within close earshot, an outburst of five fast beats before the pace lessens, with the occasional double tap in the looser bars that follow. What rhythm is this that he is pounding out for me; what is the message in this distinctive avian syncopation?

It is a familiar sound, so at first I just take it in semiconsciously—*sapsucker, uh-huh*—but then my auditory cortex really starts firing and I realize that there is no longer a big tree standing where the sound is coming from. The old pine, probably for many more decades than I have lived the preferred punching bag of this insistent bird and his forebears, died last year, died as if in the name of making the favorite window by which I sit—where I work to try to find my own rhythm, tapping on my keys—into the sunniest one in the house. If no pine remains, then what is he using as his sounding board? *Oh, shit*; I think I know.

This time it's not the house (the occasional male woodpecker loves the responsiveness of siding-as-big-bad-drum when he is announcing his territory in spring). He has chosen a particularly choice young pine tree, *Pinus bungeana*, or lacebark pine, a tree grown not just for its long-needled pineness, but for its very distinctive, colorful, camouflage-pattern bark that peels away to just get better in time. Or not.

In characteristic sapsucker fashion, the bird has pecked a perfect grid of holes into the bark of my lacebark pine, rendering it more Peg-Board than the random beauty of texture and color I (and the tree itself) had in mind. On the big old pine, this was no imminent worry; that tree, taller than the house and with its multiple trunks, could stand up to the pressure, though it, too, was eventually weakened. On my young lacebark, it is tragic, and I know that the tree may either perish from its hungry attacker, or at least be severely disfigured when the oozing sap dries on the dead tissue beneath, a large swath of blackened mess.

"You have to go all Annie Oakley on it," says Dennis, a local nurseryman friend I ask about anything that befalls my woody plants here, since they are his area of great expertise. As in, get a shotgun, girl, and shoot the damn bird. Of course I will not, and Dennis is teasing me, knowing that; this keystone species, as it is called, opens up the holes that other birds without the strength can then drink from, too, so pesky as they are, sapsuckers are a critical, foundational part of the community and I am not the queen who has the final word (nor a scepter, or even a shotgun).

There is the momentary fantasy, though, at following his suggestion: If I am not mroach@marthastewart dot com any longer, I could try out for a Wild West show, or perhaps the rodeo. I have the supply of leather jackets—I could glue on some fringe—and always did like at least the idea of chaps, particularly on Scott Glenn. *When I was a young girl, I had me a cowboy....*

Besides the insistent sapsucker and occasional head-on collision, this spring, the second of my supposed freedom, is just too quiet, at least in all the meaningful ways. I thought that our basic rhythm—the big bass drum of a collective, pulsing life force— was restored for at least a moment when I heard Herb go up and back for coffee at the diner a few reassuring days last week, but then there was not another sound from his direction. There was a relapse; another surgery is scheduled.

Same with the website: Somewhere, way deep inside in a dark and secret spot nobody can find, a bit of vicious code has been deposited, and every time we think we've chased it out and take a breath, up it comes again, mocking us. I am becoming a layperson expert on cross-site scripting and SQL injections and other nasty-sounding tactics of digital destruction—researching for any tips in a bizarre world where the mission is to take hostages in the name of spreading the gospel of Cialis and Viagra in a tongue I do not speak—and I am sick of it, as sick as Herb is of not being able to get his vegetables in.

We've fallen and we can't get up.

There are no toads falling from the sky here, at least not yet; who knows what plague the next scene in the drama will deliver, though.

Splashed across the bleak canvas of my thoughts right now, my thoughts of Herb and of all my hard work gone hacked, there are flashes of brilliance, moments of light. There is no rain all month, which is not good for the garden but yields some lipstick sunsets, as the singer-songwriter John Hiatt would say; some real pips (my father's favorite expression). And there are all these birds, sometimes right on cue with the celestial fireworks, like the male *Icterus galbula* (the Baltimore oriole) and my friend the tanager—one tangerine, one the hottest scarlet, both dramatically splashed with black—whom I catch drinking together, less than a foot apart, at the frog pool's waterfall late one afternoon. Life is tinged with splendor.

Someone, though not me, is already making use of the lounge chairs UPS delivered yesterday for the patio just outside where I sit relentlessly at the table of my impromptu situation room. The pair of cheap knockoffs of the real Italian deal—I know myself better than to spend much on outdoor-leisure items—is my first such furniture in all the years here. Why bother, I have always figured; when I am in the garden, I am working—I do not sit, and never recline to nap or sunbathe, but I keep pretending that someday I will. Good that someone else has taken an immediate liking—*splat!*—to the new mesh recliners, but *who are you, dear unfamiliar bird*, all tropical-looking with that bright yellow belly and flashes of cinnamon-orange in your wings and that long tail, and *why have we never met before?* Look how your olive back feathers match the chair fabric perfectly. Am I a decorator, or what?

The flashy bird turns out to be the great crested flycatcher (*Myiarchus crinitus*), a denizen of the treetops; no wonder with his love of the upper reaches that we are not better acquainted. *What is he doing here?* It will be many weeks before I figure out his attraction to the stone patio, which he visits over and over— and which is also where I find the sheds, or cast-off skins, of the snakes who live in the walls just beyond. This jumbo flycatcher likes to line his nest with snakeskins if he can get them, and apparently I carry the best local supply. *Our pleasure to serve you, sir; do stop in again soon. New deliveries arriving all the time.*

My senior frogboys are up and at 'em, at last, fully alert and starting to vocalize, at least the first erratic utterances they offer before the real chorus begins when sex finally fills the air a few weeks hence—or at least frog sex, as we are already rife, and ripe, with bird sex here. At night, the peepers have a steady gig, but not the bulls, not yet. Now it's just the odd belch, so unpredictable that my ear's not yet tuned into it, the way you cannot catch the beat when the orchestra is tuning up in the pit, even though you are in your seat and ready for the music to begin and start to soothe and seduce you. The metronome remains broken, like the calendar and the clock. And then, we somehow manage to go further out of tune. One night, the bulls are simply gone, though I do not realize it right away.

That next day I am sitting on the stone patio outside the window where I usually work, not far from the cat's winter shitting grounds, talking to a neighbor who has stopped by, something that happens almost never, because someone has to be very bold to dare slide my sixteen-foot-wide metal farm gates open from the shut-tight position I keep them in. If this rare visit hadn't occurred, I might have remained oblivious awhile longer. The way our chairs—the great crested flycatcher's chairs—are facing, we can see the lawn between the two frog ponds, the smaller one just to our left and the larger one several times farther in the same general direction.

Christine notices first, though innocently, without grasping the meaning: "Oh, look, your frogs are hopping around," she says, as something (*boing, boing, boing*) catches her peripheral gaze. *Huh?* I am thinking as I see the hopping, *they don't do that; that's a one-way street and they're going the wrong way.* And I stand up and walk into the grass, which needs cutting but has not yet fully dried from a giant storm two nights before, a storm that dumped two and three-quarters inches of rain after all those weeks of none, and I see them: several small frogs hopping from the small pool to the large one, a place they simply never go, and for good reason.

Frogs must have a caste system of sorts, probably formed because frogs are violent, and seem to know that other frogs are, too. If you know what's good for you, babes in frogland, you don't leave the ghetto that's designated for your kind. Ever. Like birds and so many other animals, they observe some kind of pecking order, and here at the center of my (the?) universe that expresses itself as three tiers or classes, always observed strictly and always matched up with the three sizes of water features near the house. Two oversize seasonal troughs by the door are the favorite summering spot for really tiny frogs, ones just meta-morphosed from their tadpole life phase. The small inground frog pool of perhaps eight feet across is for the small-to-medium frogs (the ones who are hopping happily across the lawn *in the wrong direction* now). The twelve-foot-wide pool, also twice as deep as the smaller one so perhaps 1,800 gallons capacity com-pared to 800, is where the big boys hang, period; year after year, for more than fifteen years, nobody strays where they don't belong, a self-policed segregation I do not understand except to say it's some form of survival mechanism, a pragmatism about *staying alive, staying alive.* Mess with me, and I will eat you alive. Sounds like the city where I used to live and work.

The big pool, for years now the domain of size XL bullfrogs and the biggest, bravest of the green frog species (those perhaps age three and older), is a jaws of death for smaller frogs, who just stay politely put in the pondlet twenty-five feet away. Mice don't know the rules, nor do chipmunks, so the bulls grab any such furry beasts they desire that scurry by the bigger pool; rodent tartare, devoured headfirst. Salamanders—those shy beauties—are not safe; even the occasional bird flies in a fatal feather's breadth too close in search of a bath or a drink. If the big boys are at poolside, pretending with their motionlessness to be invisible, they lunge—their sticky, giant tongues coinciding with aggressive bodily movement toward the incoming visitor. Only the strong, and the strong stomached, survive here. I feel ill.

So is this a kamikaze Jim Jones mission—was the Kool-Aid green?—or have all my little ones gone mad, like the birds in the window? And so I follow them, the few human steps it takes, and instantly realize I have been deserted. These relative pipsqueaks are moving, because they can.

All my big old boys are gone, five of them—the survivors of the March skunk attack, formerly a six-pack, the ones too sleepy then to have been up on the melting ice at that fatal moment. They were born here, and each one had been with me as many as four years—because yes, I can tell them apart. *Seen one frog, you haven't seen them all.* My friends are gone, and the little ones are grade-schoolers graduating to middle school today, or maybe they're the Jeffersons, suddenly *movin' on up.* Oh, right: *Nature abhors a vacuum* (though I doubt Spinoza meant amphibian nature, specifically).

I feel completely and totally abandoned, and as I stand in the sunshine here, I think about crying. But no; I must be missing something; this cannot be as bad as it seems. I pretend to have it together, but then once my neighbor is gone and I can gather myself a bit, I go and count carefully, instead. Six frogs seem to be in the big pool now, or no, perhaps it's seven: five who are green frogs (*Rana clamitans*); one leopard (*Rana pipiens*); and a solitary one-year bull (*Rana catesbeiana*), not tiny but only one third the scale of the guys who left this apparently useless under-age female behind with me, an apparently useless over-age one.

Where have they gone? And why? It is the week before Memorial Day, and I am five bullfrogs short of a full deck, among my various liabilities.

FORMER PRINCES IN THE MAKING, also known as frogmen I have kissed, have been knocking on the door again lately, though not thanks to the matchmaker, who seems to have vaporized beyond the occasional perfunctory e-mail re: "still looking for a great match for you," his vanishing act a fact for which I am prob-ably relieved. If this job of looking at myself and what I have amounted to were not so strangely consuming—I who used to do everything for everyone, doing only for me now, and really more *being* than *doing* at all—I would probably be angry at him, but there is not anger right at this moment to be mustered.

I thought the vintage-red-truck-in-the-driveway episode would be the last I'd see of my ex-husband, but no: An e-mail just flew in with a link to an online slide show of his latest paint-ings, and after I looked and sent a courteous and positive if not totally engaged reply, another e-mail came right back:

"I just wanted to show off a little."

The Pilot is rattling his cage, too, if not mine as thoroughly as he once did, from across the world, the e-mails his only way in at all since I have unfriended and de-Skyped and unfollowed, unbuddied, and otherwise silenced any routes that the master of peripatetic partnership might have flown in the window through again. From the remote island where he is stationed in the Peace

Corps, there are holiday greetings, and repeated thank-you notes for employing his daughter (I did not throw his literal baby out with the bathwater, no; she proved the silver lining of the mess). There are happy birthday messages and photos of his new surroundings (I think that's what the jpg's show) and who knows what else; I quickly scan to see if anybody's dead, then toss the lot, and try to catch the Buddha's eye again. *Forgive me, Buddha, for I have sinned—but hell hath no fury, you know, brother?*

Apparently Flyboy reads my blogs, has subscribed to their attendant weekly e-mail newsletters *(um, why?)*, and finds an irony in the tiny legalese boilerplate type at the top of each edition: *You are receiving this e-mail because of your relationship with Margaret Roach.* He cuts and pastes it into another message and off it heads my way. He was nothing if not clever—oh, and a big, fat cheat, and my hogshead of real fire, as in: *Over men and horses, hoops and garters, lastly through a hogshead of real fire!*

And then we go from digital expressions of our midlife desperation to 3-D manifestations again—the matter of a handmade cherry table leg that arrived by FedEx yesterday, packed in a green velvet pouch inside a foam-lined shipping box, like some museum piece, with a note inside bearing its provenance, something about an episode from a New Year's Eve the better part of a decade before.

We are all having our midlife transition, me and my various exes, but I, for one, am not spending mine calling or e-mailing back into time past. Time present is enough most days, much more than enough, and I am working on the occasional glimpse of time future. Bygones, sleeping dogs, all that stuff—farewell, my lovelies; peace out. So why is everybody writing to me now, Woody Allen? I suspect if anybody knows, it is you.

The sender of the table leg is a furniture maker, the leg one interlocking piece from a prototype he'd given me one holiday season, when I had traveled several states away at his invitation to spend the long New Year's weekend together. What had seemed like something of a breakthrough—the holiday weekend together, his idea—proved to be a breakup, instead. It was our second or third time around over many years; the risk had been high, but this time, he had seemed to want it. I thought I did.

Furniture Guy and I didn't complete each other the way his table leg and its top and sides did, we learned, when he announced that this "just can't work." (*Can't or won't?* I could hear Dr. Goudard saying to him, had he been present at the festivities that night. *Can't or won't?*)

A fire was going in the fireplace that New Year's Eve night, I remember, and there was expensive alcohol, slipped from the freezer where it lay waiting to be poured on the pain, hidden in its frost-encased bottle, then drizzling out of the pour spout in that thick-seeming way booze that's very cold does. Cold was apparently the theme: Not incidentally there was a record blizzard that would prevent me from grabbing my possessions and driving south again—the awkward, unwanted, but trapped guest.

No, I couldn't go until the region got dug out, adding injury to insult, and so we sat for a night—*Happy New Year!*—and some of another day, mourners over a bloody corpse, feigning civility. I finally left, but not until he insisted on stuffing the gift in the back of my Saab, an ancestor to the one I now drive. The corrugated box contained the pieces of the original, handmade table that kicked off a style now in production, the prototype. That "in pieces" part is important—a joke on someone, and that might be me. This very talented designer's patented stroke of design genius is a system of building high-end knockdown furniture—stuff that comes apart for easy flat shipping—but doesn't look shoddy in the usual KD-furniture way.

I blame the long drive and all the frogs before him and also Lucinda Williams for what I did next. Whirring nonstop in the slot I'd shoved them into in the dashboard, CDs like hers can make a mad girl madder. By the time I got home I had already scripted the letter in my head:

In the spirit of deconstructing things, as you chose to do with our relationship, I am sending back your precious table, one piece at a time.

It got worse from there, behavior that I usually don't display, or at least never had until that tipping point in my personal breakup history. *One breakup over the line, sweet Jesus, one breakup over the line.* Into a box went the first lifeless, wooden body part and the letter, and though I never continued my promise (the rest of the prototype's pieces remain in the box in my attic), the act invoked years of two-way silence.

I never knew what happened to the leg; perhaps it found partnership with parts of another table? Oh, no, the note this week revealed. Not at all.

"The table piece was not something I stuffed away in the back of a closet," the card explained. "I placed it in this velvet bag, put it on a shelf in plain view all these years to remind me how awful it feels when I was careless with the heart of someone I cared for deeply."

Apparently Old Boyfriend Season is officially open, and like all the seasons and the signs, it's supposed to be telling me something. Something, perhaps, about how many times I tried and failed, and then tried again? *Must I remember all this right now?* Yes, I guess I must.

After all these months staring out into the eyes of Buddha, a glimmer of an aha—I know one thing at least: My various serial relationships, all my do-overs and fresh starts, may not have yielded a lifetime partnership or anything close, but they did do something I must have wanted or needed then. Starting over, and over, and over created the exhilarating illusion of eternal youth, of not really getting any older, since every few years or so there was newness, the sense that the world was all in front of me again. These days, newness does not derive from drama around "the other," but from the conversation with self, from merely sitting quietly and bearing witness. I was then—as I am now inside my big metal farm fence with its sliding doors—my own gatekeeper, emotionally, physically, and yes (*nod to Jonathan*) increasingly on the metaphysical plane as well. It's up to me what gets in here, or what's cast out; it always was. I just used to sell a lot more tickets to the performances in those old days than I feel the need to lately.

Now and again I guess there will be a little revival of scenes from all my old shit, and the shit of those I have known and loved, stories usually filed away in the vault but now—*thank you, gentlemen*—each cycling its way up to consciousness one slide carousel of glimpses at a time—*click, click, click*—as my empty schedule and silent days and comfortable seat make room for them to be viewed and heard. *Attention! Attention!*

Chapter 5

The Giddiness Wears Off

An' here I sit so patiently
Waiting to find out what price
You have to pay to get out of
Going through all these things twice.

—BOB DYLAN, "STUCK INSIDE OF MOBILE
WITH THE MEMPHIS BLUES AGAIN"

IT'S RAINING HISTORY HERE, and I am feeling a little trapped. People from the past are pouring in, at least to the e-mail and the post office box, and therefore into my head again. It's suddenly begun raining madly outside, too, as if it wants to help wash away the past, erase every drop of it (especially the nastiest stains), sending it all downhill and across the road and into the brook below where it can just keep washing and washing until it's somewhere far away, maybe in the ocean, eventually, and flows around the world.

It is a Noah's ark spring-into-summer, a hundred-year event (just like the economy; a time of drama and hyperbole on all fronts colors for my first *sola* year, it seems), and each day of added torrent and torment since that first storm that dared my dear bulls to bolt, it musters the pure gall to rain again.

By mid-June I have had nine inches in two weeks, then it gets to be thirteen in thirty days. (For perspective, that's about one third of the average annual local rainfall, all in a single month). And on it goes. This year's giant pink puddle of rose petals forms beneath the rose climbing on the garden shed, whose blooms have begun to shatter in the ceaseless storms; extravagant beauty born of impermanence.

Buddha doesn't flinch, and the remaining frogs don't seem to notice, either, all sitting just as statuelike, whether it's simply *Hound of the Baskervilles* out or absolutely teeming. I have never seen more slugs or larger ones, a fact of the food chain that means that not just my amphibian friends are fat and happy, but so are the local reptiles.

Usually a sound particular to the humid months of high summer, I am growing accustomed early this year to the long phases of *hummm* and then the shorter *whooshhhhh* noise of water being collected from the basement air and timbers and next expelled into a sump situated almost directly below my chair. The work is being done by the serious dehumidifier, the one that this year runs not every so often but nearly all the time. My garden is drowning and there will be no crops of many kinds; good thing I am not really a pioneer in the wilderness and the food co-op with its bins of bulk everything and vegetables galore is only twenty-two minutes away as the Saab flies. One thing after another in my sodden domain is besieged with holes or lesions from pests or diseases.

Have mercy, have mercy, baby, their botanical voices seemed to be telling me, and so out they come; I am yanking one after another of the diaper-rashed infant victims or acne-covered adolescents and composting their soggy, pocked remains. The most experienced gardeners know this one thing about keeping up appearances, at least, in bad times: Bury your dead, and fast. Why have to look into their last-gasping faces a moment longer than is necessary? *Human kind / cannot bear very much reality.*

No, the first two sowings of squash have rotted; the bush beans were eaten by someone as soon as their first true leaves emerged; more than half the sweet potatoes simply seem to have decayed in place, any evidence of their normally vigorous vines suddenly vanishing, one sprout after another. Bulletins from Cornell University make the national headlines: The earliest and worst U.S. outbreak of the blight that caused the Irish Potato Famine of the 1840s is ravaging the East—another hundred-year event, or worse—so there will be few if any tomatoes, and their cousins the potatoes may be taken, too.

But the one thing I could do without (at least do without seeing every time I take a step, if not literally live without) is ever so plentiful: We are having a bumper crop of snakes.

The giddiness of my new life, it seems, is wearing off, and frankly I (jobless, scheduleless, and incomeless though I may be—seemingly without encumbrances or restrictions) am feeling increasingly free but also completely trapped.

I still cohabit this body with my old friend the agitator,

but it is gentler now, finally; for that I am increasingly thankful. Even if it does jolt back onto high—this spinal column of energy, this *sushumna* or kundalini, this snake—a surge of residual electricity sizzling upward and putting me into hyperactivity, it's all my own stuff it's making me do. I am no longer a commercial laundry into which others put coins and get results. I work a lot, usually seven days, though not for money; in fact, I work more than I ever did when I had a staff of 150 people, and a seemingly longer to-do list, a digital appointment book packed by fifteen-minute increments until it, and I, burst. Funny that I still hear in myself this craving: *I want to be somebody.*

I just come downstairs, put on the tea, and start to work—as if that will answer the nagging *who am I if not...* question—rarely stopping until the same hour but followed by PM has passed, or longer. Working always did provide the answer: AVP, VP, SVP, EVP, *somebody* meant somebody with a rank and the increasing esteem and dominion, like in the military. That's all still in here in this old house, with me, that *I want to be somebody* energy. I love my crazy projects—the garden blog and now another, a blog network about all the meanings of the words *sister* and *sisterhood*—and the writing I hope will someday become a book, and working in the garden, and all of it, and I am driven as ever, self-propelled, agitating but not so agitated any longer. I need to make money, but I also need to *be somebody.*

I have been shaking off the phrase "didn't work up to potential" since my first report card (and the part about "doesn't work and play well with others" was always a bit of a nuisance, too, come to think of it). But now the unspoken, unwritten admonition is delivered straight to me, from me: Am I a has-been, because of the actions I chose to take in coming here?

I prefer to think I am an about-to-be, in spite of my un-spring-chickenness.

But here's a wrinkle: Between the depth of the rumina-tions, and all those damn snakes beyond the walls, I feel stuck inside the house, unable to cross the threshold without a ritual of carefully checking to see who is waiting for me, and often even that doesn't guarantee my passage anywhere. Most days I do not even open the farm gates down by the road; to outsid-ers I appear a self-imposed shut-in, I am sure. "We thought you were away," neighbors say on the rare occasions they see me at the post office (where at every holiday, a table is spread inside the lobby with thematically appropriate cookies and cider or eggnog and even a neighborly bowl of dog biscuits). If only I were Ben Lee, I'd simply belt out "Catch My Disease" in way of explanation: *My garden is a secret compartment / and that's the way I like it . . .*

To be clear, by "depth" of ruminations I do not mean dark-ness: in fact, there is so much light in here, at my wonderful seat—light and happiness, even, just not exactly the jump-for-joy kind you go out to party about. I am not bubbling over, but I do awaken every morning with a vague feeling that it is a childhood-era Christmas, a day when I will open gifts, and though I may not get to play with everything today or even know what all the presents I've been given really do, exactly, and will need to grow into some of the goodies among them, I still feel happy for the haul.

It has been a very long time since I did what anybody else told me to do.

Yes, the giddiness has worn off—it is no longer my "new" life, but just my life, now that I have completed not merely a second spring but half a second year, now that I have anniversaried so many of what last year were first-time experiences, the thresholds or rites of passage everyone was watching to see me cross (wondering if I'd stumble and head on "home" to the city).

These are the maiden voyages of the *Queen Margaret II*; my fresh restarts. So far the only passage that's got me really stuck is made of a thick slab of oak and slathered with solid-color stain the same shade as the house, the darkest olive. It's the threshold to the outdoors, the one between the kitchen mudroom and the world.

Jack, too, is afraid of this particular threshold, a trait I have seen in other cats but do not exactly understand; perhaps the behavior that birthed the word *scaredy-cat* is at work? He will often jump it altogether, after much sniffing and hesitation and usually a few electric twitches bordering on backflips, rather than actually step on the wooden saddle that forms the boundary between in and out, between the Big House and the Great Outdoors. Me, I just hesitate—and often then retreat.

This, he and I are here to tell you, is one tricky sill.

Jack is a threshold animal: neither tame nor wild, as happy (I assume) on his all-night prowls across the road outside the human realm as he is in the hours on the pillow here beside me while I work. I get it. Yes, the pillow—that's right; we have both softened. Once the only pillow was in his cabin beyond my doorway; by last winter its look-alike had earned a spot in my mudroom, where I feed Jack each morning and evening. Gradually, in a four-step progression, he has sucker punched his way to a pillow right beside my feet, the pillow a flying carpet that has now finally landed. I am still not a cat person (*she doth protest too much*), but I am a Jack person, at least.

This threshold is giving me fits, too, Jack; I am wondering who will be curled up on it or just beyond, where I cannot see, wanting to gain entry when I try to gain exit. Me—the big gardener, the nature girl—but lately I just want to stay indoors, and cross the threshold as infrequently as possible because of my incessant awareness that the serpent awaits. "The serpent is transformation," a certain increasingly irritating doctor notes one Tuesday evening on the phone. "It's a fear of letting the wild things in—and also a sign that you are not done with being, or feeling, trapped." Oh, be quiet, you (but yes, of course yes.)

The dreams have begun again:

I am at a fairground, in the ladies' restroom, when another woman comes in with something wrapped in a plastic sandwich bag, the way you'd scoop up poop if walking a dog in the city. But she has a small snake in the baggie, and is going to put it in the trash. "No," I say. "Let it out!" And so we do, and it is on the water-splashed, well-worn, tinsel-flecked fleshy-pink-colored Formica counter beside the sink and it starts to mutate like something in a fantasy animation film from Pixar. It puffs up, and lots of undulating tentacles dotted with every possible color like that palette on your e-mail toolbar where you can colorize your type burst forth from various points on its skin, small colorful fireworks of brilliant colors, all from the one little snake. A rainbow, right here in the ladies' toilets. It is magical.

I wake up thinking of Shelley Duvall's proclamation in *Annie Hall*: *Transplendent!* Indeed, it is. Transplendent.

"Are you afraid of letting the wild things in?" says Dr.

Goudard, Mr. Troublemaker and the big downer, who'd probably like to talk about *schlangen* (the German word for snakes,
um, and the source of that slang for penis—schlong—which,
Herr Doctor, is sometimes just a snake). He points out the stark
contrast between the way I live inside—the sanitized life lived
staring into a computer screen—and what lies beyond that door.
Uh-huh.

I haven't seen any rattlers yet this year—*giftschlangen*, the
Germans say, when referring to a venomous snake, the prefix
striking me as very odd and perhaps better expressed as *nothank-
youschlangen*—but every other manner, yes, even one new to
me called the smooth green snake (*Opheodrys vernalis*), a striking
bright green creature whose scales are not noticeable (hence the
"smooth" of his name). My uphill neighbors have seen the similarly smooth-scaled eastern ring-necked (*Diadophis punctatus*), a
shy, nighttime prowler that we almost never catch a glimpse of,
though technically they are always among us, year in and out.
This summer, even what's normally hidden is on parade. *Strike
up the band.*

But no, *nein giftschlangen*, not yet (or at least not in my backyard). Certain of us talk in hushed tones at the post office or
town gatherings about the latest sightings if there have been
any—the big one who crossed a certain road the other day in a
particular spot, or slept curled beside someone's parked car elsewhere for the entire afternoon each day one week and then was
gone—but it's not something we do when anybody's listening,
because poaching (and also simply impulsive killings, reactions
from the heart of fear) happens if those who live among the
snakes tell just where, and when, to find one in any given year.
The snakes' secrets are safe with us.

It has been a year since the rattler told me to stand back, to go (retreat?) inside the house and mind my own business that July evening on my way to my ex-LA friends' home. *Get thee to a nunnery*, he apparently said, in snake. I know that the males are on the move again now, away from the hibernaculum in their rounds of nighttime summer hunting, and it feels like only a matter of time before we meet again, *some enchanted evening*.

These thoughts have made the very threshold of my doorway to the outer world a place of ritual: I do not move across it lightly this time of year, nor without scanning my surroundings with a systematic, cautious eye. I peer though the outer glass door, and then I swing it open, and then I peer again, and take just the one careful step. And then I stomp to announce myself, because snakes do not have an outer ear or inner eardrum to "hear" with in our human understanding of that word, but instead feel vibrations with their special hinged two-part jaw (which of course is normally on the ground, all the better to catch vibrations through).

All my stupid screaming didn't mean a thing to any of the snakes I came upon all these years; it fell on the equivalent of deaf ears. A good, firm stomp at least signals my approaching presence. And so I am a cartoon character in my box-shaped red Birkenstock clogs, stomping around in an exaggerated manner, sounding the take cover alarm for all my reptilian friends.

"The camera can make it feel less scary," my closest female friend, Erica, a professional photographer, told me, seeing my new gait, and advised that I start looking through a long lens at the various non-*giftschlangen* species who brazenly sun themselves everywhere and even try to slither in the back door if I am not alert when opening it. Apparently this is how she got through shooting some particularly brutal journalistic assignments in years past. I have been forcing myself to look with this extension of my eye, to take photos of them. And then I force myself to crop into those photos on my computer afterward and really, really look: at the hot-colored tongue that flicks and flicks and flicks again to pick up the scent of potential prey; the jaw with its amazing hinges; the eyes each a round black bead encircled with a ring of rich, deep amber; each scale an ingenious part of the bigger pattern that is the paper-thin skin that must regularly be cast off in favor of the new.

But again and again, I retreat to the safety of the reference books to find something that will help me feel at ease, playing to the comfort of intellect rather than the feelings all of this provokes. Facts have always been my magical thinking; if I put enough of them in my pockets, like Hansel with his crumbs, I can walk a few steps farther into the woods. And so of course one recent day when I was needing a dose of intellectual courage or at least an explanation and excuse for my terror, there it all was, in the *Journal of Evolution*, the factoid of all reptilian factoids, the herpetological mother lode: Ninety million years ago, when the early snakes evolved to be able to constrict and therefore achieved the ability to prey on primates, our primate ancestors fought back by taking an evolutionary step themselves—by developing improved eyesight, specifically by developing forward-facing eyes.

Apparently being outsmarted by their supper was something of an inconvenience to the snakes, and so in time they got themselves the fact of venom, about sixty million years ago. Next move by the primates: enhanced all-around vision. *Take that!* And so on. The reptiles got trickier still, and our earlier kin adapted with color vision and pattern recognition (and who is more patterned than *giftschlangen*?), all because of the snake.

Um, evolutionarily speaking, snakes helped us to learn to see: to see what's ahead, and also all around, and all of it much more clearly—staying safe all the while, out of harm's way, knowing just what to fear.

I guess that was what Jonathan was saying all the time. Go look for some snakes, Margaret, and let them show you how things really are.

ANYONE WHO VISITS SAYS IT SEEMS LIKE A CANVAS of *Peaceable Kingdom* or a scene from Animal Planet at my place, but I am here to tell you otherwise much of the time; maybe the locals just behave for company. Particularly in the rough times of high summer, there's a whole lot of fighting going on. Since my big bullfrogs departed for better digs during that heavy rain in early spring, the species called green frogs have been full of themselves, self-appointed masters of the universe, and now with mating season upon us, they're downright violent. Ever watch a frog fight?

Green frogs (*Rana clamitans*) live an estimated maximum of six years in the wild, reaching sexual maturity in their third year and top size at age four or five. In May through August in my climate, females lay one thousand to seven thousand eggs on the surface of the pools while being held in the romantic frog embrace called amplexus, with the male fertilizing the eggs as he grabs on to her. The males get dressed up in yellow mating-season colors; the female doesn't even bother to don a cute new outfit, so maybe this amplexus thing is all about the guys; who knows?

In the season of free love, what's all the fighting for? World domination, apparently, or at least domination of my little world here. In green frog culture, the lead male calls in the females with his booming voice, which many amphibian guidebooks liken to a loose banjo string being plucked. But I love the story of the underdog, er, underfrog. The so-called satellite male is an opportunist, waiting and hoping that Mr. Big's voice lures some cute chiquitas who won't mind a consolation-prize date with the vocal also-ran. Shades of post–Velvet Underground Lou Reed: *Satellite of love...*

The guys are fighting, pretty much nonstop; shows occur from lunchtime onward into early evening. I could sell tickets. As I watch, though, I keep doing the math—wondering what happens to all those many thousands of eggs times all the females who live here with me. The surviving eggs (ones that don't get eaten or otherwise perish) hatch into tadpoles in three to seven days, but tadpoles don't begin to metamorphose into full frogs until a not-very-precise range of three to twenty-two months thereafter, meaning tadpoles may even overwinter, waiting for the moment to feel just right. Amazing. It makes me feel like I am right on schedule; this life-change stuff takes time.

On and on they fight, for days on end, and then, like everything I start to count on lately, or at least begin to understand and grow accustomed to, the scene goes and changes on me, though even I was surprised at the next round of antics. Apparently tired of daily strife, one of the male greens climbed up more than three feet from the pond surface to reach the wall where the Buddha stands. Pondering his next step, it seemed, he turned and looked back, and down over the edge, to see from whence he'd climbed. Perhaps he was reconsidering the whole idea of scaling such heights? But no, after all, *I am going for it!* Up the rest of the Buddha's shoulder he made his way, and there he sat for more than an hour, as if whispering into the good lord's giant ear.

It seemed the frog would stay in his posture of quiet communion forever, but then the heavy commuter traffic picked up. The local chipmunks began high-speed shuttle service across the wall, including a stop on top of Buddha's head; up one shoulder and down another, *but oops, there's a frog on the tracks!* Hard to find any peace with so many chipmunks around; *I hear you, frogboy. I hear you.* But we must try, despite the incoming; the speed bumps; and yes, even the steaming piles of you-know-what.

Whose shit is it, anyway? That's really the bottom line, I suppose, to all this ruminating, all this retelling inside my head (yes, and sometimes out loud) of my story, at this more-than-midlife juncture.

Whose shit is it, anyway?

Someone not so long ago said that the statute of limitations on blaming one's parents was long over—ah, yes; it was Gordon Livingston in that little hit book, *Too Soon Old, Too Late Smart*, in these precise words (yes, I managed to find something in the living-room book maze): "The statute of limitations has expired on most of our childhood traumas."

The longer I sit here, the more I think the same is true about the one on blaming your ex-job, ex-spouse, ex- or current anybody. If I stayed a day too long at the fair, at any of the fairs I have been to so far, that was my decision, wasn't it, just as the moment I walked away was of my own making. I have always loved the sound of the word *volition*, the reminder that power is within us to move right, or left, or not at all. (Perhaps I should drive a *Vol*vo instead of a Saab?) Now I am here; let's get on with it, Margaret. *You are free*—and not free as in that infantile definition I once held, all those months and years I was waiting to accumulate some magic number of dollars or some such, not as in: *Don't worry, everything will be taken care of, dear.*

Volition. *Vroom*. And there is another *V* word in the air.

The price of freedom is eternal vigilance, Dr. Goudard says his own therapist has always told him, a paraphrase of the Irish politician John Philpot Curran from 1790, but often credited to Thomas Jefferson. Curran said similar words on the topic of the right of election. Forget to keep a sharp eye out, and you will serve again: a master, your demons, something or someone you don't wish to bow and scrape to any longer. Now Cheese tells me the same message, the latest in a loose chain of wise men passing down the wisdom of their elders in the best tradition of mentoring. There are always things to watch out for, even when we have made the best-laid plans.

I know the thought was not original to Jefferson because *I have the time* these days to look everything up, and so I do. I am a fact-checker, though not for hire. No longer able to pass the hot potato to another person for my stuckness—there is no boss, no supervisor—I have gone to Plan B of psychological procrastination: I delay the next bit of my momentum by looking things up to "understand" them better. *Uh-huh. Right.* Important work, this research, and mercifully (when you have an empty calendar like mine), it's so wonderfully time-consuming. But I am blessed—or maybe it is all magic, after all: A guide always appears to tap me on the shoulder, just in the nick.

As if to remind me of my mission, a large animal is suddenly in my sight lines, out the west window—the stage for my inner play, where everything seems to be revealed to me—eating apples under the farthest old tree as if it's his yard, his orchard, his kingdom. Doesn't anybody know this is my kingdom, and I am busy right now? Do not all assume that because I never leave this chair, I am not engaged, booked, fully occupied. Would you all interrupt someone who was kneeling on a prayer bench or seated on a *zafu* in meditation?

Is it a really big red fox, or a small coyote? Or could it be a gray fox (*Urocyon cinereoargenteus*), the animal from whom the dog is descended, I think, and one (though not rare) I have never actually seen except in books? One way I might figure that out is if the animal has shit while gorging himself on my windfalls. Yes, that's what apples that leave the trees early are called: windfalls. Doesn't nature have the most loaded words for everything? I've got myself a windfall, and somebody probably just shit on it.

I must get my molded red clown shoes on and go on scat patrol, trying to ID some droppings, as if it's not enough that I suffered through Jack's end-of-winter sale on the stuff. As if it's not enough that all the boyfriends have sent theirs along lately; or that I am still here trying to identify whose shit it is that I am still feeling I need to shovel, turning it over piece by piece, figuring out what's next in my increasingly not-so-new new life.

Where the hell is my scat reference guide when I need it? I know the keys by heart, though: ends tapered, or ends blunt;

continuous or segmented; diameter and length; color and (*ick*) contents. *What is this particular pile of shit made of?* In fall, for instance, some animals who are normally more carnivorous or at least technically omnivorous will binge mainly on sugar-rich fruits, taking on a temporary madness as frugivores. A bear's scat in fall or a fox's will be laden with seeds and colored more like the dark juicy berries he's been eating than some meathead's (laced with skin and hair and bone bits) would be. Okay, I am going out to locate and assess some scat, and then I will be right back, to work on more of my own. Will this crap(ping) ever stop?

Yesterday all I had done was step off the back porch on my way to get some salad in the vegetable garden when someone tried to get my attention, if a bit more passively than this canid is doing today. A long, slender ribbon embossed in great textural detail, like some semitransparent, tubular mosaic, was woven into the grass right beside the stoop, its glossy surface picking up light and catching my eye.

Yes, snake, I know; enough with the hints. It's definitely time to shed some skin. Did that damn Jonathan send you? I can hear his tone, see him practically wagging a (loving) finger at me, nudging me with little dares across that threshold my ridiculous boatlike shoes seem magnetized to, anchoring me in the midst of what has been.

You have a shamanic way of seeing the world, but you have such a resistance to step into the metaphysics of nature.

Because I didn't listen to the birds, frogs, cat, snakes, light-ning—because I just didn't listen to any guide, human or otherwise, or even to myself, or if I was listening I didn't inte-grate what was heard and then take steps to action, at least not yet—they're circling the wagons, surrounding me with messages, beating their drums together with a quickening, everlouder frenzy. Of course, it is a soul song they are singing: *We are family, I got all my totems with me. We are family....* But it is also the Jonathan type of soul:

If we honor our gifts, Margaret, awareness will arrive, and we can live with more congruency, closer to our true self. Pay attention to the signs, as they say.

Shut up, Jonathan, shut up. I am paying attention, I want to say, in self-defense of the woman that I was / am: the one who lived that life but also knows her botanical genera and species, who can tell not just plants but also the various reptiles and amphibians apart from one another, even the boys from the girls; who can key out a respectable number of birds and works on IDing animal droppings and footprints in the snow. Oh, the pattern that the birds make after a light snowfall, so many *Y*'s in mad, silent, and ephemeral avian hieroglyphics—an ephemeral cave painting that John Burroughs called the stitching on the coverlet; a favorite part of every snowy morning—his and mine.

Doesn't that count for something, Jonathan Ellerby, PhD? Don't I get any points at all for at least intellectual awareness?

But no, finally, it is sinking in: The same trait that kept me in the unwanted-but-familiar groove I was in for so long—the nasty lifelong habit of living too much inside my intellect—is now keeping me from making a new groove here, one with edges just rough enough that I can wriggle into it and use its contours to scratch my way out of an old skin, exposing a brave a new one. This will take some nonthinking. It is a time for aesthesis—for pure heart exchange with other living creatures—not intellection; a time to dowse for meaning but not perform an engineering study en route. Be still, my beating brain. Stop thinking.

That's it: That's the answer. I need to go a little more out of my mind.

OH, SHIT, HERE WE GO AGAIN—in my now you seem 'em, now you don't life—just as soon as I start to gain my confidence in reptilian photography, they are gone. I had been gradually moving closer in to get better and better shots of my companions and maybe starting to enjoy this rush of courage and daring, and they are gone.

But now the head that I had come to expect and regard as my daily photo op is no longer poking up at nineish each morning from that precise space between two particular coping stones capping the wall around the patio. A large garter snake (the one who ate a beloved frog right in front of me) had hunkered down in the cozy space for weeks and weeks, between its outings for sunbaths or snacking, and every morning I'd look out at the appointed time and there the yellow head would be: *Up periscope.* The smaller one who lived a few cracks down seems to be gone, too, and so is the pair on the frog pond wall beside Buddha, and the big loner in the compost area, alongside the asparagus bed, which has transformed itself into a frothy fernery after a succulent April and May of firm, crisp pickings. All gone, or at least not in view—and certainly not forgotten. (Perhaps I stomped too much, sounding an evacuation order rather than just a friendly alert? I am new at this.)

Now, now that I have finally gone to look and try to see, not scream, I cannot find a snake despite my considerable patience and visual concentration. We can long for, and miss, even those whom we at first wished to turn away.

No time to lament the departures here, though: The new arrivals (perhaps the passengers unloaded by some unseen docked craft during all that rain?) are making themselves known, and rudely so; there would have been no way to miss the latest sign served up for my viewing and pondering pleasure. Because I did not listen to the snakes, or anyone else who preceded them in my litany of guides disregarded, apparently they sent a skulk of gray fox—yes, that was a gray fox the other day, and in fact I have a group of them, which is known as a skulk (she says, using another factoid as ammunition against fear). The foxes in turn have delivered their own message: a "scat latrine."

Today Susan mostly watched as I shoveled up what was the contents of a scat toilet fashioned by my fox family, who converted into their personal lavatory a flat spot in the far reaches of the garden that was mulched but otherwise unused. This is where Susan, *schlangen*-friendly and generally the braver of the two of us who work here in the garden—she who snips slugs in half with her shears—loses it. She carries away dead bodies Jack has left as love tokens, but doesn't take any shit. Some things disgust even her.

The sixty-or-so-square-foot area was mulched with clean straw—or at least it had been clean until now, until my new friends the gray foxes decided that this was their giant litter box, and deposited dozens of piles of scat in the one place, seemingly overnight. But why? To mark the territory where they are feeding happily on a seemingly endless supply of apples that fall to the ground—my windfalls, remember? Even if we pick up every fallen fruit, these clever canids (unlike any other dog relative but perhaps one) can actually climb trees to pick the hanging fruit themselves—or to elude a predator, or even just to take a nap, up and out of harm's way. Unique claws put it all within their grasp. They know a good thing and my place is it, so they mustered all that shit in a hurry to say: Keep Out; Skulk in Residence. They may even be marking a nearby den or resting spot, where they are curled up during off-peak hours catching a few winks. Oy. *How do I like them apples?*

No wonder we have not met before, as the gray fox is crepuscular: neither nocturnal nor diurnal, exactly, but hunting and most active during the betwixt-and-between hours near to dawn and dusk, the hardest times to see. Yet another liminal creature has made itself known to liminal me. Today I am shoveling fox scat and fouled straw onto an old bit of tarp that we will empty in the woods and then dispose of, and I am ripping up an old men's undershirt into strips, tying the impromptu white ribbons to dozens of bamboo canes and setting those with a well-placed thwack of the hammer into the earth of the scat toilet I hope to reclaim and remediate. My desperate handiwork looks like so many flag-topped pins at a really miniature mini-golf course. And then because all that preparation so far has merely been my vehicle for pheromonal warfare, I am opening my bottle of very expensive coyote urine and saturating each little flag with the strongest pee I have ever had the misfortune to encounter, pouring it into the cap then letting one streamer at a time wick up the dose of piss and turn dingy-colored from it, all the while trying not to spill my precious elixir.

Shit on me? Oh, piss on you!

I will repeat the shit shoveling and surrogate urinations daily until I come out the winner, succeeding at pretending to be top dog in this test of dog species; the wily coyote am I, at least in spirit.

Who am I if I am not mroach@marthastewart dot com any longer? I am now a rather obscure category of restroom attendant, and I am not sure that I really want the job, which in this dump does not even feature tips. Even I am not prepared entirely for just how much shit there is in this one lifetime to clear away, or at least make sense of, but I keep shoveling.

"Survival Is the New Success"

Before I know it, it is August. Jack and I are both shedding, though winter is far off (at least by the official calendar for the Northern Hemisphere). Not skin, admittedly, but hair, a bodily product rich in its own symbolism from personal power to sexuality to who knows what. I could look it up and tell you, but I am supposed to be resisting the impulse to retreat into intellection now, aren't I? The heat, which has finally risen to at least a brief summery blast, has us both molting, which some species of birds are doing, too, partially shedding their so-called alternate plumage or feathers (like hair, also dead tissue) for their basic ensemble, the one they wear in the off-season when nobody's showing off to get laid.

Everyone off with their siding! (Yes, little house, I know— lately you form what has become one of my own protective layers as I sit tucked inside the wrapper of you, with both of us safe inside the big metal fence at the woodland's edge. Help me exfoliate, won't you? Do something to coax me across that doorstep of yours.)

My brush is full each time I wash my hair, the only daily ritual that has not been lost, the one I still honor by letting the late Victorian-era sunflower showerhead rain down on me in anything but low-flow style as I stand stark-raving bare on my antiskid rubber mat in the giant claw-foot tub. I pull the strands out gently from the brush's bristles afterward, a daily source of simple accomplishment and tangible result, *tada*—like mowing, like shoveling snow—and ball the harvest up in my palms, before tossing it in the white enamelware waste bin that the Martha Stewart catalog sold before it went away. Many strands are gray now; like a duck gone all dull after mating season ebbs, this is my eclipse plumage. I remember scoring the vintage-style covered can on markdown, during the closeout, but I treasure it. It makes a stylish and strangely sentimental receptacle for my used Kleenex and Q-tips and wads of shed hair; a collectible from that life I cast off that now collects the latest editions of my life's debris.

Jack's brushes are full, too, and then some, a hair-clogged range of devices from basic to serious that I use to groom him at varying frequencies. The gentlest one is inflicted several times a day to show him that I am the top cat, the dominant animal here; he must still submit to a brushing to get fed, whether breakfast, dinner, or the little treat we have added at midday. (Jack does not know I am also top dog; I do not pull my coyote rank on him, though I suspect he knows about our recent uninvited guests.)

I need to be in charge of someone—me: *Marge Roach, The Boss*—as my father's father wrote with white chalk in his Victorian script on the locked door of a painted blue stepback tool cupboard in the basement of my childhood home. Grandpa

Roach, John Lewis Roach specifically, had been a master carpenter, his specialty the hanging of large doors such as those in churches. When he'd come to America in 1898 he'd hung his share for upper Manhattan's houses of worship, before becoming a chauffeur for the Philip Morris Company's founding family. As his first grandchild and one named for his late wife, I was the only one allowed to open the cupboard where his planes and chisels were stashed along with every manner of specialty nail. I was the boss; it was ordained so early on.

Fast forward: "You are too bossy," a long-ago boyfriend said in explanation of why we could not go forward, and especially why he would not live in a shared space with me. "Too bossy, and too neat."

And then there were the Martha years, my pinnacle of bossdom. Now, though, there is just Jack to manage, and he is at best recalcitrant, at least when he is awake.

It is August. One female bullfrog, a mere girl when those five males left her behind in search of real women and bolted in early spring, is now grown to a young woman herself. She swims alone in the bigger pool, remaining skittish around me, true to her breed. A week ago, I held the last nearly metamorphosed green frog tadpole, bearing all four legs but also his withering tail, which he shed soon after, or more accurately resorbed. Its color was different from the rest of his body, somewhat lifeless by comparison; not the green of growing things but a lifeless brown, the way more of my hair that once had amber and auburn flecks like gleaming tortoiseshell is now gone increasingly silver in the mirror and in my brush.

I wondered, looking at him in my palm, if he took the slow road or the fast lane to life on land. *Are you the Tortoise or the*

Hare, Mr. Frog?—was it three months, or nearly two years? The oldest male green frogs have stopped humping each other, stopped calling, stopped caring; it is August. I like the feeling of their temperatureless skin, and the awareness in my hand of how (though smaller) they weigh more than the unexpected harvest of stunned birds I sat with in earlier days. There is a density or gravity; a heft. They give not a shit, and in their new centeredness or Zen state they are fine about being held, their reproduction frenzy ebbed.

I keep feeling as if I, too, am over the hump. *A time to embrace; a time to refrain from embracing. / Turn, turn, turn.*

The good Dr. Goudard says no, another someone's on his way, and the high-ticket matchmaker sends more of his occasional e-mail messages of encouragement as well, the "not yet but soon" variety—probably just so I don't make a fuss and demand a partial refund, the skeptic in me says. I feel so determined to catch up on all the years lost to others' biddings to even entertain the thought of another distraction, or at least I think I do. At this very moment, on these steamy, sluggish days when the air does not move, the folly of chasing sex seems like an awful lot of trouble to me and my frog friends. Only sitting still on the immovable spot—whether by the bodhi tree or in the dining room—gets you somewhere. Perhaps all those months living under the watch of Buddha, the One True Boss, is some explanation as to why we are at least temporarily in possession of our centers, with some sense of equanimity.

Since his mating instinct slipped away a week or two ago, one of the males of the green species has taken up residence on the back porch, just near the door, and when he does utter a sound it is disconcerting to hear it coming from *there* (the porch) and not *there* (in the water). It catches the attention of my right ear and not my left now as I move on the most familiar path I travel here day in and out, dumping food scraps into the compost, picking salad or green beans, heading out to mow. *What are you doing, mister?*

Frogalicious.

Do you want to come inside?

A tiny green, just metamorphosed a month ago with the last round of graduates from the aquatic-only life, is over at the kitchen door, a cunning decoy set up, it seems, to help me get over my ritual *look-step-look* thing that has been the troubling, year-long echo of the rattlesnake. I still hesitate at the threshold between in and out, though this charming little amphibian, a mere inch long, has me almost forgetting and semifearlessly kneeling in the doorway (at snake level) to speak to him; I find him irresistible. No surprise to me that frogs apparently speak a remarkably similar language to the one of cats, or at least here in my world they do.

Things are shifting, and with them my attention; I am no longer the keeper of great armies of frogs, my beloved amphibians, the creatures of double identities (amphibians, from the Greek words *amphi*, for both, and *bios*, for lives). I am no longer the person of both lives, either, so perhaps this is why they are not calling to me so urgently now, the way they have done every year until now of our acquaintance. I have not driven south to the city in two months, skipping even my ritual haircut, seeing no one from that old time and self and just hunkering down here to try to do some metamorphosing of my own. I guess the frogboys know that I, too, am bobbing with no particular direction in sight.

It is August, and the rains have returned with a vengeance, putting mowing off schedule again as it did in the great flood months of June into July. Once again the too long grass that I cut when it was also too wet (adding insult to injury, but I had no choice) is rotting in place—a smell of decay is underfoot.

With the frogs and the birds gone mostly silent, the percussion section of my backup band is manned by the apples—the windfalls—which drop with a hilarious *thwunk* at will, night and day. Danger: *Don't sit under the apple tree with anyone else but me.* If Susan and I tire of picking up the hundreds and hundreds before each mowing or simply miss some, there is also a smell like apple pomace wafting upward from the vast swards, an aftermath of cidering and not typically of mowing, a smell out of place and time.

In the midst of all of it there were garden tours—a public open day, one of two or three I host a year for charities, this time to benefit the town and the park that is its primary attraction. After the hundreds were gone, someone fell asleep in a chair that night at eight. The fat American toad waiting at the door the next morning (loyal old tight-lipped friend that he is) was not saying who. He was just happy to be able to show himself and move about once all the incoming feet other than my familiar ones subsided, and not to have to hide behind the pots or under the stone barn steps for another day. It's all a blur: the season, my life here lately, the tour—but there was the one man who came up the walk from out of the crowd with hugs and kisses to deliver, an old, lost friend surprising me—and, um, was that a flash of heat I felt? No; it cannot be (over the hump, remember?). I'm exhausted, as is the garden; it is August.

The string algae on the bigger pond is hot to the touch when

I go to tease it out from the surface with my hand, feverishly hot. A green percolating mass has brewed itself—*Double, double toil and trouble*—like nothing I have seen in all my many years tending these little water worlds.

If like the big toad we are looking for signs underfoot (thank you, John Burroughs; thank you, snake), then the resounding message is that something's festering here in my corner of the world, or at least starting to brew and bubble up, depending on whether I'm in a half-empty or half-full mind-set. Say that we haven't moved past shit to putrefaction, and that this is more a test tube about to offer up some answers than a pending eruption, some explode-in-your-face experiment gone bad. I think so, I really do; but then, it is August.

ALL MY SOCIAL SKILLS AND COPING STRATEGIES ASIDE, I have the spirit of a lone wolf, a heron, an eagle—or perhaps a spider. I do not travel in packs, and never really have except for earning purposes. Even as such, I must admit that I have joined the larger community in deepening ways these last months, almost in spite of myself. Opening the garden for the public fund-raiser was part of it, yes—but strange as it may seem, mostly the sense of belonging began when I spontaneously took hold of a spatula and began flipping a few boxes of pre-packed burgers the other evening.

I hadn't planned to do the cooking when I headed down to a spot beside the state park manager's home—my next-door neighbor, technically, though our houses are nearly a half mile apart—to attend a potluck barbecue for a new friends group formed in the park's support. I hadn't even planned to stay very long at all; just to bring my tray of marinated, skewered shrimp as a donation to the cause, sit awhile, and then wander back up the hill and inside my own gate. But a bigger-than-expected turnout meant a production line would be needed to get everybody fed—or one very fast chef manning the grill.

"Who's doing the cooking?" I asked Ray, who runs the park, and when I heard his "I guess I am," I said, no, you have to welcome all your guests; let me. In taking on the burgers and dogs and buns and even my tray of shrimp that night, I think I provided not just a steady flow of food, but also some of the entertainment. But this act of improvisation—*let me cook the burgers and dogs, Ray*—that seemed so natural to me was a surprise, and a hoot, for everyone else, owing to my Martha Stewart provenance, I guess, and also probably to the fact that a number of key people in the group know I haven't eaten meat in many decades and probably spilled those beans. Photographs of the act were recorded; maybe I can use them in my résumé.

If I am not a successful publishing executive anymore, I am at least a pretty efficient short-order cook; *that's one rare with cheese on a toasted bun; well-done coming right up.* A girl needs a job to survive, right?

Survival is the new success. A gleaming yellow postcard bearing this message arrives from a former business associate, David, and looks so very much like another omen, or at least an affirmation—the perfect antidote to any doubt. It earns an immediate and prominent spot on the windowsill, facing in, a sunny reminder to just keep going, something's working, or at least being cooked up.

Or maybe for me it's not mere survival but the right of self-determination that is the blue ribbon in this race we are all on?

It has been more than a year—since the end of the consulting phase of my transitional Martha agreement in July 2008—that I have done what anybody told me to. Imagine that: Marge the Boss of Marge the Boss. *Chalk one up in the win column, Margaret*; let's celebrate these newfound metrics for success in your frog-eats-slug (not dog-eats-dog) new world.

Or is it how many weasel tails you end up with, because if that's the new success metric, Jack and I will surely be victors. The count from his summertime hunting stands at six now, arranged in size order on the arm of the folk-artsy, quasi-Adirondack-style chair he lounges in when I simply will not let him indoors, just outside the window one third of the way between me and the Master's stone countenance. The chair, one of two scored in the prosperous years at an annual garden event in the tony nearby part of Connecticut (in my *I'll take those* days), was long ago painted the most horrid and also wonderful shade of pale green, like someone added a little white pigment to the bucket of chartreuse high-gloss enamel (bad idea). Its gouges and scrapes reveal earlier incarnations as something much tamer and cream-colored, and then also a lifetime that immediately preceded the green one: a violently happy yellow phase, the primary yellow that your first pack of Crayola No. 8 Gold Medal School Crayons would have contained, the crayon you made the sunshine and its rays with. The chair and its mate fit right in here with me and the house and even Jack, who like the rest of us is gradually reverting back to earlier layers of personality I expect he displayed when he was a house cat in someone else's reality.

There are other triumphs and trophies in my marathon solo event, like the end to that vague dread of Sunday night that pervades the working wounded, who if they were like I was all those years also want to stay up and eke out some sense of "mine-ness" when they get home from work each weekday evening, despite being all in from the events of the day; the constant tension between the desires of the I and the other—*pushing, pulling, pushing, pulling.*

These days, whatever the night of the week (admittedly, I do not so accurately discern one from another any longer), the approach of bedtime is cause for excitement, something looked forward to. Though I am neither retired nor employed, another aspect of my betwixtness, there is none of the anxiety that I brought to the beckoning comforter and pillows when I had a job in the conventional sense. Sleep is not the enemy—no longer a block of time you don't have time for—nor the thing to be crammed into whatever space is left. Sleep is increasingly peaceful, pressureless, and pleasurable.

If I awaken at three or four in the morning and choose to read awhile, no cause for tension; I have nowhere to be but downstairs, and there only because it's where the teakettle and refrigerator are situated, since I will crave something from both eventually. *Whenever I get there* will do—a feeling of indescribable luxury, the lifting of some decades-old negative association that made bedtime into badtime.

Not so long ago, Mondays were the brutal reentry; Tuesdays better than that, but by then the race was really on. Wednesdays were the middle child, the spine of the mountain that was the often-rocky workweek. Thursdays were the big push, because if you didn't go into hypergear and get it all done, Fridays became synonymous with late-night drives along dark but familiar roads, hurtling to the country, wishing it were earlier and that your precious hours there hadn't already been picked away at by someone else's timeline, by your commitment to work for hire and all that such an agreement entails.

No, I love the ritual now of bedtime (and how convenient to find myself dressed in sleeping garb again when another day winds down); love the evenings leading up to it. The waning hours are like licking the spoon of cake batter, tongue darting between the beaters' unfastened upturned blades, a hint of the cake-to-be's flavor even if the shape and texture isn't quite there yet. Tasty, and so deliciously tempting; my unbaked life has all the right ingredients. Yum. Not so long ago, it took much more to thrill me: the exhilaration of a new relationship, a promotion, one of those spa trips, a binge at Saks. Now it's just the advance guard of tomorrow—a little taste—and knowing that today was mine all mine.

And then I take in the delicious concoction that is morning. There is no hurry, though, and that last fact has needed all these many months to really register in anywhere but intellect, for it was obvious from the first full-time day but not really understood. There is nowhere to be but here. For decades I awoke moments before the dawn—no alarm required—a farmer's soul inside a corporate soldier's body; awoke with an urgency that I must hurry to steal some quiet for myself before the day stole all the peace from me. Nobody is stealing anything now, and if I roll over, I will not lose my little share of today, for all of it is mine.

Not the lottery top prize, perhaps—and still there is no real steady income, the bank statement reminds me each month. Despite the fact that I must now, for the first time in this adventure, dip into savings to indulge myself in keeping at it, there is a richness to these days, and I hear Emily Dickinson's voice when I think about why: *To comprehend a nectar / Requires sorest need.*

No bonanza with blinking lights and bells, though certainly newfound delight in each awareness of the pleasure derived from something once hurried through, barely conscious, or even loathed because its thorny, insistent quality dug into places that were hard to let be touched then. The most tender places had to do with time, and how much of it was not my own. My sorest need was to slow down.

My yoga remains lost, despite a few near restarts—no further run-ins with Céline Dion to report, but no more than a stretch of four or five classes, either. Even without the ritual of asana practice, without going through the motions, though, my yoga is never very far away. A meditative quality has infused so many things; I cannot help but notice. Living as a constant witness to nature will do that to you, instilling rhythms without the intervention of alarm clocks or BlackBerries (uppercase *B*, though the lowercase kind will tell you what's what, too, if you get in a tangle with them). My once essential handheld device lays idle here, sitting by the power strip, but like the unneeded alarm clock upstairs it's now ticking off hours, minutes, seconds that don't have the same currency they once did, since things no longer move at that same cadence, or seemingly even in that time zone—or was it warp?

Music, too, particularly music with words, continues to strike me these days as without utility; I am listening for other sounds, and there are plenty.

Nowhere do I see the change more than in the way that I approach tasks related to food: growing vegetables, cooking, tending to the shopping and to the tidiness of the kitchen. In all of these, I am mounting my own slow-food movement, a one-woman, one-mouth-to-feed effort. Long a seven-to-ten-a-week consumer of pre-packed frozen organic dinners, I haven't had one since I started my sitting practice at this dining table with the view—so long ago that the other day while I was food shopping, their real estate in the food co-op's freezer case evoked the reaction of not "staple" but "sinful," just like the nearby ice cream.

I have my hunger back. I think of all those many thousands of workdays when the assistant of the moment would ask the question even the assistant had grown to detest hearing: *What shall I get you today for lunch?*

But I had lost my taste for all of it—every sushi joint and deli, and every franchised faux restaurant that Midtown Manhattan had to offer its weary workforce, and the ultrafancy ones we went to for meetings or to entertain business associates, too. I wanted none of their possibilities, but now, in my simple little kitchen, I stand awestruck, refrigerator and pantry closet doors ajar, and dream of what it all adds up to. Polenta competes with orecchiette for my supper's foundation, or will it be quinoa instead? And what of the accompanying sauce—something based on my garden tomatoes, maybe?—or homegrown garlic and something green (pak choi or brussels sprouts or chard or kale or collards or bush beans) and some delicious local cheese?

"Margaret lets the garden tell her what to eat," Sara Kate, a blogger friend who visited recently and wrote about me said, and she was right; it does, and to the palette I add every color and shape of beans and grains from my once-every-ten-days run to town.

Only three meals today, Madame? I say (perhaps out loud), the sound of lament in my voice. Damn. So many things look good. *Roach, table for one?*

I waste nothing now, shuddering to think how much didn't survive my back-and-forth life, forgotten in the wrong refrigerator, left to fester into science-fair projects in the wake of my neglect. Ah, to simply walk across the room to your own refrigerator for lunch—and also to enjoy everything: the ritual of cooking for and serving myself, and in it evidence of self-care; of knowing who the boss we must each serve really is. *Or else.*

I grew my vegetables carefully this year. They, too, were treated to a fresh start, with tractor-bucket loads of compost from the heap and appropriate amounts of lime and organic fertilizers added in to every raised bed in early April, even before the first lettuce or pea went in the ground. Even then, in the cool of not-yet-spring, my spading fork unearthed a tangle of earthworms of baby snake size proportion—I grow them good here, though I am probably the only gardener of my standing who still recoils at their wriggling gait. Happy to have such a bounty, but *gross.*

Other than my new fashion nonstatement, the way I garden and the way I then cook show the change most clearly, because the gardener and cook has nowhere else to be. When you are chopping wood (or carrots—or growing them), just chop wood. Delight in every movement, and become it. There are moments of something approaching weightlessness, and even mirth. Just yesterday, I took an old red bike from the barn and just pointed it downhill: Regression in progress; I'm hearing you, John Hiatt (and did you write that song for me?): *Old days are coming back to me. . . . But I had nothing to live up to and everywhere to be.*

I have my hunger back, and I don't just mean for food. *Who am I if I am not mroach@marthastewart dot com?* I am a woman who increasingly basks in the quality of just enough, and not a pinch more. That in itself is quite the abundant blessing.

Chapter 6
Trying on a Myth for Size

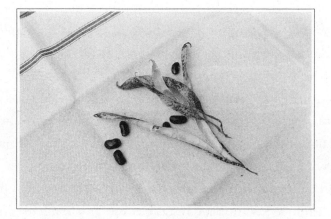

SHADES OF 12-STEP: Let's stop looking things up, Margaret, and take a searching and fearless moral inventory, instead, what say? Or if maybe not an inventory, exactly, why not just play a game of connect the dots and try plotting the series of points representing one visitor after another these last provocative months—a frog here, a fox there, a lonely table leg over there—and see what is their cumulative shape?

But I don't know exactly where on the page I'd place what things I have witnessed, really, relative to one another. I have neither artistic inspiration nor the defining device of a graph—no framework with two clear axes, except the actual axes out the windows where I stare, and stare some more, at pictures formed by literal seeds I planted, now full grown. Along the southern sight line, on the hill above the Buddha, a copper beech dragged up there as a baby now boasts a trunk that is bigger around than I am. To my west, beyond my right shoulder, a diversity of shrubs consort with one another, and with the ever delicious possibility that another sunset will backlight them on fire.

What I feel in need of so achingly these heavier days, when the dew stays longer and longer beyond the morning and afternoon must fight mightily to even overtake it, is not a man or a job. There is finally equanimity on those scores, and nobody is more surprised by that fact than I.

Increasingly it's not even the evening wine I desire, but simply to put down my story of me: my myth, one that I can grow older with in comfortable style. Since the old one no longer fits—like the wardrobe hanging in my closet, a vestige of a life left behind, it just doesn't resemble me any longer—I need a story of myself.

Hopefully I can do better in my own behalf than to merely tell a tale of a woman who enters a garden where many serpents live and old trees are heavy with apples, which all the creatures including herself want to eat. Those are the facts, or at least some of them, but not the myth, not yet—and *hmmmm*, I think that story's been written, hasn't it? But yes, it is a personal myth that I must conjure, for little by little it becomes clear: Brewing it is what I am doing here these months and now, startling as it is to realize the fact, two thirds again more than a year.

"We are all myth-makers about ourselves," May Sarton wrote in 1968 in *Plant Dreaming Deep*, when she was fifty-four, the age I was when I came here to be with my true home, "but part of growing up is the shedding of one myth for another, as a snake sheds its skin. I have no illusions about ever becoming a true countrywoman—there is too much behind me of a different kind."

Sarton typed that bit about the snakeskin while sitting alone in her house in a rural northeast village, a house whose worn old floors were painted yellow (like mine have been since long before I read *Plant* the first time, and also the follow-up *Journal of a Solitude*, from 1973). When she looked up from the page, it was to look out the window at the bird feeder and the garden she so loved growing all around it. Sarton sat down to write each day only after she had wiped the kitchen counters and made her bed; only after queuing up her most familiar albums of classical music to usher in the muses if they were willing on any given day. She had Albinoni, Mozart, Vivaldi—and yes, Bach, too, the only music I really play anymore, at least for now. No Romantic composers, Sarton said; at least not for writing time—give her music with structure. And she had regular visits from Perley Cole, who appeared as if by magic from down the road apiece and helped with chores—armed with scythe, not chain saw admittedly—and also with good conversation.

My bed is made. The kitchen's steel surfaces—engraved with every errant slice I've made into some vegetable or other in decades of hurrying to process the whole garden in just two days a week and missing the mark—have never been cleaner. Of course we are alike in these small ways, not just in the bigger passions of garden and the greater landscape; that is no coincidence but just the statistical and mystical reality of there being only so many kinds of us humans in this enormous world, present and past. She is as much my ancestor as is my own sister, or at least spiritually speaking—my treasured, if imagined, old friend. At some intangible level, we share a lineage. I would never have enjoyed conscious awareness of this fact if not for a one-two punch by Sydney Schanberg, an ex-*Times* colleague who thirty-odd years ago offhandedly said, "You would like May Sarton," and then Dr. Goudard (who gave me *Journal*). Thank you both.

I just knew, for instance, reading her phrases again recently, that Sarton had read *The Hero with a Thousand Faces*, Joseph Campbell's 1949 masterpiece about myth that influenced so many who have tried to grasp and then perhaps even retell the story of a hero's journey. *We are all connected.* I knew she had, because in my latest attempt once again to research and think my way out of a moment of prolonged discomfort by studying and taking notes, I'd opened Campbell and dug in myself, and then traced the subject back a little farther in time, hoping to find the instruction manual for successful crossing to the other side. (*The raft is for crossing over*, the Buddha would pipe up and remind me now, *not for clinging to*.)

And Campbell had been part of a lineage, too: Campbell himself had been influenced by the work of Arnold van Gennep of Dutch and French ancestry, whose 1908 *The Rites of Passage* claimed that three distinct stages—preliminary, marginal (or liminaire), and postliminaire—were part of each such ritual that marks any major change in life phase; there are no shortcuts. (For Campbell, the phases would become departure, initiation, and return—a difference of phrasing, perhaps, but there was still no way around any one of them. Sorry.)

After Campbell, there was Scottish-born Victor Turner, an anthropologist, who eventually expanded on van Gennep's middle phase—the threshold itself, the betwixt and between, the very time of liminality. Some of its qualities, in Turner's way of thinking, ring with a startling familiarity: Expect to be subjected to tests, seclusion, and sexual ambiguity when you are on a threshold, he said; you will be humbled. (And if you are a group, you will experience communitas, a sort of unity outside the society—while roles are all up in the air during the transition, you are all just one. Think of teenagers, who are neither boys nor men—unripened pumpkins, green tomatoes. Within all liminal individuals or groups there lives the germ of something new; the opportunity for great growth, Turner said.)

I did not know when I undertook my optional change of life that there were so many theories I could choose among or adhere to. And once I found the first (thank you, Joan Borysenko), which led me to another, and then, *dot dot dot*, there I went along that path. From literature and mythology to anthropology and even physics and chemistry—the work of 1977 Nobel chemist Ilya Prigogine, for instance, and his theory of dissipative structures; and have I failed to mention Carl Jung and his work on individuation? I could have stayed in research and thinking mind forever, reading about how structures undergo transformation, though hopefully not remaining on the threshold in perpetuity myself as a side effect. There are volumes of humankind's musings on the time between no longer and not yet; it is our most essential fiber of connection, our common lot.

You are not this body
You are not these thoughts
You are not this ego

Mine is no new story here, except that I am the character in this particular enactment as each of us finds ourselves to be in ours. Even without a proper education, this dropout soul knows that much. I was taking Greek mythology at New York University the second time I left college, one of several-bordering-on-many times. I was in my second semester of studying English and American poetry then, too (and living in the age of Jim Morrison–channeling–Aldous Huxley–channeling–William Blake), so Blake's circa 1790 "doors of perception"—*For man has closed himself up, till he sees all things thro' narrow chinks of his cavern*—are imprinted way inside me. I think it was one of few courses I paid enough attention in to ace. The undercurrent of mysticism in Blake and for me even more so in Yeats and Eliot was what grabbed my attention, about the only thing from all those years of my "failed" education that stuck.

With my imperfect and incomplete schooling, I cannot really know what it all means—the poems, the psychology, the philosophy, the physics—but no matter. I go now, as then, on such glimmers of commonality and understanding—*Eureka, I am not alone!*—grabbing the gestalt I can grasp and then moving on to find the next link in the chain, the next clue. A meal can be had of such mere bread crumbs of awareness—of this I am certain—and they can even be fashioned into a map if you are really wanting to go somewhere. There can be found a sense of great and needed belonging even in unknown voices from the past or elsewhere as far away—or here and now, if not personally known to me. "It is exceedingly likely that my greatest success is behind me," *Eat, Pray, Love* author Elizabeth Gilbert said in her 2009 speech on creativity to the TED Conference. I hear you, sister, but I also hear that it's okay.

I look to make sure that there are others like me, find comfort in their journeys and the uncanny similarities, the startling onenesses that come just as you need a boost, like little miracles. This is maybe why I don't feel so alone here ever in my rural residence, the way others feared I would when I said that I was heading to the woods: I have the words in all those books out there in the other room; the lines emanating from the wi-fi radio during nonwriting hours, or Gilbert on the YouTube clip, or a particularly well-timed and phrased blog commenter; the play unfolding outside my windows under the direction of the talented and experienced Nature. The signs and signals seem to say it was all put on for me, to help me across the threshold. Don't we all have to believe this to feel that we belong, to root ourselves in and keep growing, particularly as we age? Even in physical solitude, there can be community of the spirit.

Sarton, a prolific poet and writer of fiction, also wrote journals—to come to terms with herself, she said in interviews. She did not explore the journal form until this age—my age, this "midlife" that's not a midpoint at all. She sorted herself out, I see now as I reread with an older eye, with the process of recording those reflections.

But sorry; I grow ponderous, and anyway, *what was that?* A splashing sound far bigger than any frog could make, and now beneath the Buddha I can see a chaotic fountain effect from the water's surface, waves on the surface of the little pool. There is a woodchuck in the frog pond, a woodchuck paddling madly doggie-style, his fur plastered to his oversize rodent face and body, the Goodyear blimp of drowned rats. He's fallen in, and he can't get out. Even the poor, definitively terrestrial wood-chuck is trying to show me his other side—an aquatic one—as if in empathy for my own neither here nor thereness. Do I feel mercy, or any community with him?

Just last night I had seen the woodchuck, the first (miracu-lously) this season to try to set up housekeeping in the garden, when he sauntered up the front path at about five PM as if to say, *What's for dinner, hon?* I wished him dead, and when I failed at the required and all-too-familiar systematic search for the entrances to his burrow so I could set a trap and begin the tricky capture process, I went inside and wished him dead again, and had a drink.

Be careful what you wish for; a giant rodent is drowning right before my Buddha, directly in his sight line, and I am not sure what I will do about it. And then, like so many things here, he is magically rescued: saved by Susan, or at least by her timely arrival for the garden workday and what peer pressure does to turn my inaction into active lifeguard duty. Together we do a garbage-can-and-fishnet routine and scoop him out, and she drives him down the road apiece before she says farewell, and probably also this: *It's nicer here than at Margaret's, promise. Margaret is a positively inhospitable bitch to woodchucks, you know. Consider yourself lucky.*

Who are all these visitors in my solitary life and what roles are they playing in my story? Because I am no artist, and also as I say not well versed enough in any of the theories out there— not in Campbell, Turner, or van Gennep; not in the shadow, anima, animus of Jung the way that Dr. Goudard would be from his training; not the beneficiary of decades of teachings from a Native American shaman, as Jonathan has had the fortune to be—I have no choice but to propose a theory of my own. How will I tell my story, especially to myself; where will I paint myself into the pictures that are to come?

Hold that thought; once more, I am being interrupted. For a place that is so quiet, a lot goes on here. Now there is Jack again, standing at the porch window, cocking his head so he can see me here through the mullions of my extra-tall two-over-two panes, past the back of the chair opposite me, across the teacup and over the rims of my glasses and the laptop's upraised screen. There is Jack again, frantic to come in, to be here, not where he is; no longer wild, but not quite tame, struggling with the spiritual and actual threshold where he finds himself. There am I, reflected in the inside glass against the image of his frantic grasping, though I am sitting deceptively still.

YOU CANNOT STALL THE INEVITABLE; SEPTEMBER TAKES CHARGE. Two bubbling Pyrex baking pans of If You Are a Vegetable on My Counter or in My Fridge, You Are a Dinner Ingredient casserole are already in the oven, though it is only eleven in the morning. *Smells good.* Jack is snoring on the towel-covered pillow beside me, his white paws wrapped around his mostly black face, in from another night on the town—well, all right, the hamlet.

It is one of those days of pink dawns followed by wild, swirling winds, as if the air is the ocean and the tallest treetops the waves. Now, at nearly midday, roll and crash, roll and crash tsunamis of the surrounding forest canopy continue to lick at the lopsided opening—this hollow on the hillside—where I spend my days. Will I drown in wind, and what weather is it washing so vociferously onto my shore next?

I am cooking though it is nowhere near dinnertime because I am stalling, having grown tired of the twice-weekly mowing that the ultrawet growing season of these last months has perpetrated. I am all mowed out after hours and hours devoted to it each week since May, just to watch it all come back, taunting, almost at once. Normally mowing is required twice a week from the first week of May until about July, and then you get a reprieve—just one weekly pass needed—until September or even the rest of the season, which ends about early November. In its defense I will say that mowing is just what the doctor ordered for a person on the threshold: the delight of tangible progress with every step; no doubt which way to go, not ever—keep pushing until it's all short. *I mowed today: See, I did that. Me. All by myself.*

But there are so many ways to put off the task: by saying the dew hasn't dried yet (*never mow wet lawns* is sound turfgrass wisdom) while hoping it rains the moment the grass approaches just dry enough. You can postpone by cooking, as I am today; or perhaps by picking up the fallen apples and pears, barrowload after load, to make sauce. That takes hours.

This last one has replaced the various procrastinations employed on days before the fruit was ripe enough, and I am glad for a fresh excuse. One can only tell oneself the same story so many times, as I have increasingly become aware in bigger matters than this. Pick them up, hundreds each time, or otherwise the tractor blades will run them over (which makes a kind of sauce, too, but turfside). Do not be deceived by the mindless sound of it; bending over and again to grab one of hundreds of fallen fruits in a session is the work that makes backaches, and yes, a different kind of boredom.

"Make it a game," Susan says on the days we pick up apples together, tossing the progeny of these century-old trees, one by one, from increasing distances into the cart—free throws alfresco. Who will win?

"Get some sheep," people I have never met reply on Twitter—you see, I am not alone; there is a flock—when I lament the chore that lies ahead. "Get a goat." I don't think I could share my garden, big as it is, with any other ruminant. They—goats, sheep, cows—are all indiscriminate eaters, and it is enough to have foxes shitting on my landscape without masticating herbivores who then will need the resultant shit, piles made from my precious garden, cleaned up after them as well. I am the sole ruminant of these acres, and so it shall remain. Marge the Boss has spoken.

Speaking of shit again, there is always mouse patrol—another stall tactic, though not a delightful one, either—but this time of year, when the devils are trying to tuck in everywhere for the duration, I can busy myself for at least a while with the task of cleaning all the traps, collecting them in an old enamelware basin, one of many in gray or white that I used to collect at tag sales in the early days, and pouring a kettle of boiling water over the lot. I give them a good soak before rebaiting them with the cheapest, scariest supermarket-brand peanut butter I keep in a cupboard for the murderous task. But no; who wants to clean mousetraps? Maybe later. When the casseroles are done, I will face it; I will mow. Like driving and taking a shower, mowing is good for ruminations, so I will make the best of the hours ahead.

A shower; ah, that sounds tempting. There is something about a hot shower now that fills a craving, as delicious as the Marshmallow Fluff topped with a squiggle of Hershey's syrup eaten out of hand in the kitchen of my childhood, as good as a binge on leather jackets that filled a different, bottomless hunger that grew in me later on.

Now it is treat enough to make my way upstairs into the claw-foot, carefully turn the hot spigot and then the cold that have each been repacked against leaking one too many times with dental floss and Teflon tape and who knows what else. Then I just stand there under the welcome stream that has passed from the ice-cold depths of my 450-foot well beneath the patio, in through the pressure tank and then—making a hard left—over to the hot water heater, and eventually ascending the final fifteen vertical feet farther up to just above my head.

If I am not my old, successful self, I am at least someone who knows the simple pleasure of a day that begins or ends with one of the great inventions of modern plumbing, someone who went from a lifetime practice of taking the fastest showers on record to someone who positively luxuriates in them. Not so long ago, I could not even stand, or sit, still. I have nowhere to be these days and I have a new hot water heater; I could just go strip right this minute and stand there in the cleansing warmth for quite some time and then a few moments longer still, and celebrate that fact of my newish life.

But first, some proper gardening; the shower can loom as the brass ring of reward. The optimistic seeds of cover crops—so-called green manures—are sown strategically in fallow soil to add texture and nutrients once their top growth is turned under a season hence. They go into every vegetable bed or section of bed we clear, winter rye and giant red clover our cold-season choices. By afternoon the wind has stifled itself, and as we work to pull plants well past their prime, it is the sound of a squeaking old metal swing set—rhythmically regular, back and forth, back and forth—that fills the air. *But I do not have a swing set*; haven't since childhood in that yard with all the tulips and azaleas, the riot of color that is a typical northeastern suburban garden picture in spring. I do not rekindle that image here because such plantings burn bright for just a moment before burning themselves out until another year; I do not have a swing set (or teeter-totter or jungle gym) because I have no children, just all these plants.

The sound is the goldfinches, mostly disinterested in me all summer but now gathering in a frenzy of activity these cooler days, screaming the latest headlines to one another about the seed-laden feeder, and wanting more, more, more. The faded plants and even the sound of flocking finches are as yet unacknowledged but semiconscious signals that it has started, signs announcing the inevitable facing of facts: Senescence is taking hold as the garden's peak moment of adulthood so quickly loses ground. The winding down is under way.

MASSIVE TRACTORS, MOST OF THEM THE COLORS of the John Deere nation I live in, navigate the increasingly empty fields around me with their headlamps blazing, hoping to finish the work of a challenging season of harsh weather that will be best forgotten except as the fodder of stories at the coffee shop someday, once time has taken some of the sting out. It is evening, but the hulking green and yellow mechanical workhorses do not stop; only a small window of dry weather is forecast, and there are crops to lay claim to and stash undercover, so on they work.

It is not the first time this season that my neighbors will labor far into the night. A caravan of odd, old vehicles—some vaguely ex-military in their appearance, army green and with the look of years of brave service to their credit—follow soon after the tractors have time to gain some ground, gathering their yield and carting it back to shelter before the coming storms. One rare dry night in August, I sat up reading with them as my companions until near two o'clock, the sound of the intrepid troop more than I could sleep to. Make hay while the sun (or moon) shines, so long as it is not raining. *Carry on.*

In such a place as this a girl can quickly develop tractor envy, and I did from the earliest years, but there was always some home improvement to pay for—or some frantic trip to a spa. It was not until a year before my departure from the city that I finally drove one into my barn and parked it for the duration.

As ever, I can conveniently blame Susan, who pointed out a few years ago that *we are not getting any younger, Marge,* and that the wheelbarrow-uphill routine we'd followed until then was more and more seeming to be positively Sisyphean—and what bad behavior was it that we had committed to be punished to an eternity of it, anyhow?

We're buying a tractor, Marge, she started to say a few late winters ago, embedding my new mantra into consciousness in preparation for the coming spring, the word *we* being just one example of how she and I speak in the majestic plural when it comes to chores and money—the word *Marge* being something only she (at least since the death decades ago of my grandfather) gets away with, so *watch it.* I may still be Marge the Boss, but I know better than to bite the hand that helps me, or even talk back. Who will hold the ladder; who will tote the other end of the heaviest burdens? Who knows all this old house's and its resident's peculiarities and particulars? Only the Susan knows.

Off we went together one Friday when the snow had melted to purchase *our* tractor. No doubt the ex-farmer who was our sales representative at the dealership profiled us as a weekender lesbian couple living the dream of rural semifreedom, but no matter. I long ago gave up explaining why a smallish single woman such as myself with a chore list of such obvious heroic length would not prefer to have a "hired man" to an even smaller woman than herself. With a hand truck and the two of us, we are plenty strong, and one thing more, or two: Women stick (and we have Herb watching our backs).

The flag I now fly, or at least my tractor, is the color of Herb's; not Deere green and gold at all but the distinct orange of our Kubota minority, both machines finished in lacquer the color of the embers from that lasting fire that first connected us, and the color of creativity. I never had as much as a riding mower before this, and love the beast, but now even with a twenty-two horsepower diesel engine and a front-end loader and a mowing deck nearly four and a half feet wide at the ready in the barn, the fierce tractor envy has not really abated. Simply put, my farmer neighbors' are bigger—in terms of horsepower three to five times bigger, and in physical dimension, too, by a multiple of at least several.

But I felt better, if still lesser than, once I got a machine of my own, and it forged another bit of our loose form of community. We already had an interest in the land between us—horticulture and agriculture being close cousins—and all the tractorless years they'd always wave if I was in the yard with my wheelbarrow or cart, but this formalized it. There are other threads: Like I am, my farming neighbors are intense weather watchers, of course; their financial survival depends on an alertness to opportunity, from the timing of the first seed sown to the felling and baling of the last crops from their fields.

And so with the coming of the Kubota, at least I upped my standing in the fraternity in another minor way. I suppose I must admit, though, that this tractor business is one area—especially with certain tasks—where size does count.

FALL MEANS THE *F* WORD IS COMING, and maybe the *s* word, too. The collection of large houseplants I stage outside the doorway as the backbone of my garden's "annual color," eschewing impatiens and such for the most part, tolerates neither frost nor snow. I must bring them in, and so I rush to make them welcome, or if not welcome, exactly, since space grows short and the humidity dips as the furnace comes on to heat our false winter world, I at least say *come on in.* We have a seasonal agreement of many years standing that I must honor, since they have lived up to their part so handsomely year after year.

With them I adopt dozens of hitchhiking spiders and even more spiderlike creatures, so many that each fall I christen myself Spider Woman. Most of my accidental catch are not spiders at all but other arachnids called harvestmen, a perfect nickname at this season when I am hauling them into shelter, albeit inadvertently, as the quietest of stowaways.

I work beforehand to gently clean off each incoming pot full of clivia, bromeliads, or the last of many big fancy-leaf begonias— the largest, oddly named Little Brother Montgomery, is positively shrub-sized, higher than my waist and almost as wide. We have been together for many years; I never tire of the sight of this handsome, faithful creature. And so I bring dear brother and my other friends, one by one, to the staging area near the hose bib, not far from the back door, for the inspections and some pot housekeeping—rinsing the exterior and rim of each one, teasing out all the withered or damaged leaves and also anyone who's got themselves tucked in the many crevices—before they earn safe passage indoors with me. But I never find everyone, especially not the elusive types we often call daddy longlegs, the harvestmen. Numerous ones always manage to get across the border with their plants, in spite of me.

By the time we are finally inside, the whole lot of us, a tiny true spider, barely one-eighth inch across if that but intricately patterned in yellow and gray and black—perhaps some kind of jumping spider?—is walking blithely and bravely up my right arm. Four daddy longlegs explore the mudroom and its slate floor and woven doormats, scaling the heights of my silly red clogs, trying to get their bearings. Don't worry, guys; I will return you to the outdoors in just a minute, one by delicate one.

I cannot blame the incoming houseplants for the giant brown spider who is on the yellow kitchen floor those nights when I get up midway through sleep for an extra little meal. I don't cry out first like an infant for its mother, but I have the metabolic rate and incessant hunger of one. And there they are: always near the trapdoor to the cellar, across from the refrigerator, my restless kin.

Spiders—amazingly enough—do not scare me. More people die from lightning strikes than spider bites each year; I pick my shots when it comes to my personal homeland terror watch list. None of these are *Annie Hall* moments; I do not get out the tennis racket and go into battle in the bathroom like the jilted Alvy Singer. *I told you a thousand times*, he says to Annie, *you should always keep a lot of insect spray. You never know who's going to crawl over.* Indeed.

No, I am not so easily frightened off. I do not fear spiders but actually now that I have time to pay attention, I see myself in them: delicate but strong; agile; going quietly about their creative business of weaving a web in an often reclusive manner. And how could I not have noticed this next bit before, or at least entered it into consciousness: In true spiders (unlike the harvestmen) there is a distinctive body shape, a two-part abdomen shaped like an eight, with four pairs (another eight!) of legs attached. Eight-eight has always been my favorite number; spiders are my people.

Scenes from a Senescence

OCTOBER SHOWS ITSELF, the opening acts reminders of the facts of cold and harshness. Frost threatens as September fades, and then again as the new month begins, but the garden and I escape each time, unblemished except for the bruises on my hip and thigh and shins and arms where I have leaned too-heavy pots, each approaching half my body weight, against myself to wrestle more of them into safety each such night of our supposed doom. Before morning tea I make a stop at the thermometer to check, squinting at the readings in the darkness that increasingly greets me these seemingly shorter at both ends days:

What was the overnight minimum?

Missed us.

Missed us again.

And another time.

I have been at this game more than half my life, and this much I know: These stays of execution are not necessarily merciful; as in any other form of limbo, the forces taunt and toy with their temporary prisoners. *Dead garden walking.*

The garden, operating as I am without its customary calendar in a year gone sloppy with battering downpours, is making up for lost time. There are offerings and then more offerings, and so onward I cook. The first freezer is bulging; I long ago learned not to stand in harm's way when opening its door, lest one or another frost-covered brick of red or green or orange or pink jump out to hit me in the foot. *Choose me, choose me*, the urgent evacuees seem to say, all those pouches and plastic containers— yes, fitted with their correct lids, thanks to my early days of rehab here, my former occupational therapy—vying for their mother's attention. At this rate, the second freezer will be full soon, too, a testament to all that Tupperware and more important, to my consistent presence: Miss Margaret Roach, Gardener and Cook in Residence. I am worse than any squirrel; maybe I am a transplanted Florida scrub jay, *Aphelocoma coerulescens*, a bird who picks and then buries some eight thousand acorns each harvest season *just in case*.

The price of freedom is eternal vigilance, yes, but the return on that *attention, attention*—at least in the kitchen garden and at the stove—is what probably amounts to one fifth of the foodstuffs I eat each year on a dollar basis, since the crops I grow are my diet staples that if purchased in similar organic quality and quantity would not be cheap.

Comfort me with apples for I am sick of love. It is October, and I am making soups and sauces (both apple and love apple, as *Lycopersicon esculentum*, the tomato, was once known); pestos of all my green herbs, frozen as cubes in ice trays then bagged by flavor; pureed winter squash from the fruits that did shape up and mature. I have even mastered curry, thanks to the old friend delivered by the garden tours, an able teacher of cuisines that will heat up my winter nicely, and have become a devotee of homemade vegetable broth as well. All the not-quite-right squash, their flesh a bit insipid from the deluges and lack of heat and whatever else befell us, might not be good for eating, but cubed up, skin and all, are an enriching ingredient for my new favorite brew. I drink a cup between breakfast and lunch each day and use it as the base for soups and the liquid for my sautéed greens and such, the universal solvent, and so frugal feeling; I would do Helen Nearing and even Grandma proud. *Waste not.*

I haven't touched the brussels sprouts, seven shrublike plants standing loaded with their Barbie-size cabbage heads that would have been perfectly suited to that long-ago village on the basement playroom floor. They will be improved by a little frost, as will more collards and kale than I can recall growing before. I am still working on the row of chard, some of its leaves this year as big as a banana tree's, or one of my garden canna's, whose rock-hard rhizomes rest now in Hefty bags in the cellar, quiet and without needs until I call on them again in April or thereabouts.

Twenty-five feet of sweet potatoes and the same of white wait patiently for me just where they grew, keeping the tally of their harvests a secret, as yet unseen. Like garlic, both are grown from pieces of last year's crop, mine or my mail-order provider's. The soil that supported them since their latest beginnings is now serving as an ideal storage medium until I must offer them a substitute or else; I really push my luck, but cannot safely wait after November comes. To spare them the possibility of death by spading fork, I dig them with my surgical glove–covered hands from the crumbly soil laden with worm castings and wrigglers who tilled it, too. How worms love these hilled-up crops to frolic in, leaving behind their own goodness as another thank-you note. Onions and garlic, now cured, are still in the barn—and incorporated into many of the blocks of jewel-toned ice in the deep freeze already.

There is no time for distractions, and in that thought is where I go slightly wrong in a new way, and bruise my heart, or at least the part of it where my newly forming self-esteem had dared begin to imprint itself.

On the way back from the first rural haircut, I am crying, heading up Route 22 with my shorn locks as if it had been my wings that were clipped—a far more painful possibility, and not one to be outgrown so easily.

Such signs of adaptation to one's surroundings are marks of face-offs between life's opposing forces. The boreal chickadee's wings have grown pointier the last century, for instance, since mankind has thinned the forest, a 2009 study on the influence of logging revealed. Maybe that doesn't sound bad, since pointy wings are better for sustained flight, yes, true enough; but in the formerly dense boreal forests—where billions of birds representing more than three hundred species of the Americas breed, one of the planet's greatest remaining ecosystems—they made maneuvering difficult, so the bird had evolved to a more rounded wing tip. *These are not my beautiful wings.* I wonder if the chickadee minds its reshaped lines; I suspect they miss the trees, though only with that kind of longing that roots into DNA. Recent generations would have no memory of what once was; its echo is imprinted only in their wing tips, and on their weightless souls.

At the salon, my face had gradually turned bright red in the haircut process, a scarlet Margaret in the big mirror—a reaction my body reserves for the most uncomfortable moments of all, for pure stress. The red face is not something I experience very often any longer; I seem to have left it behind with my income and the cute outfits and all of the other trappings.

I knew from the first snip: *This is not my beautiful haircut.* The cut was good enough, the best we have in the area I am told, after much panicky pretrim research. It was one third the dollar price and one fourth the time investment of a daylong trip to the city—the latter, in this time's-running-out last bit of harvest season, my motivation—but the haircut was not mine.

Just a few afternoons before, I'd ridden my new bicycle—one with upright handlebars and a proper basket, a bike like the ones of my youth—and in the slanty light of that fall afternoon I had seen my shadow, all exaggerated, beside me on the shoulder of my dirt road. In that moment I was a girl with very long hair again, almost to her waist; an illusion—and even more so now that I have lost the oldest bits of the real thing.

The first rural haircut was a lot like losing my virginity, except I didn't dare ask the question I asked that summer evening at the shrubby, secret periphery of the local beach—*How long do we keep doing this for?*—since this time the person was holding scissors. Somehow it also felt like I was simultaneously cheating on my longtime partner, the hairdresser of twenty years back in the city. All I could hear on a tape loop in my brain was my city transplant friend Bob's voice: *You know you've really moved to the country when you have your first local haircut.*

Driving in my semidaze back north toward home—eyes trying for a look in the rearview and then another at the imagined damage every half minute, fingers pulling on one hunk and then another of the severed hair—I realize that I have reached the mental bag-lady stage. My friend Anne had described the phenomenon in an anecdote that stuck with me, though she has now been free of her high-powered corporate life for more than a decade. It was a story about being on the subway a year or so into self-employment and looking down at her shoes that were in that very instant one too many seasons out of date for psychic comfort. She had not noticed her new self fully, in detail, until just then.

Dan, a nearby journalist friend with four more rural dropout years to his credit than I, remembers the moment this way: He stuck his hand into the closet—his closet—and pulled out a navy blue jacket by Jil Sander. *Who left this here?* he asked himself. *Whose jacket is this luxurious thing?*

Yes, suddenly nothing fits here, either; nothing looks quite right or even familiar. I want to burn the clothes that I had been all right inhabiting these months, the fusion of yoga castoffs and jeans and the odd recycled bit of corporate wardrobe that could be salvaged to pair with one kind of bottom or the other on the days I actually left the house at all. I want to go home with my sad new haircut and drag them all into the yard and have a giant bonfire, or at least cut the absorbent items up into cleaning rags, the way I do every one of my mountain of the men's white cotton sweatsocks I wear that bursts a hole—butterflying onetime foot-coverer into mopping-up tool with a scissor slice down the back midpoint of the ankle, all the way down the middle of the foot right to the toe.

I am the same size as ever, still a 2, but suddenly nothing fits mentally or visually; it is all outgrown. Even if I can easily get into the getups, the old costumes, there simply is no ease in being inside them any longer. I know, I know: Like a teenager trying on seventeen outfits before going to simply hang out with the very same friends—what difference does it make? It's not like anybody here will notice. But suddenly, in that raw haircut moment, it all makes an enormous difference. The outside packaging—to which I have felt mostly oblivious these many, many months, like Anne with her old shoes—has to match what's going on inside of me.

"You have to kill off the old self to get to the new one," the sender of the disembodied table leg had said many years before in one of those compulsory holiday phone calls, in response to hearing that I was feeling a little lost over some life change or other I was grappling with when he caught me. Yes, precisely (though probably best not to attempt this by killing off my old, good-haired self one lock at a time). *Ouch.* Even in the haircut and the tears I find a silver lining when I realize that in all this time, now approaching two years, I have not cried for what I'd left behind; not until that inch and a half (I'd asked for a mere half inch, please, no more) lay on the salon floor. Shedding.

Barely three more minutes of self-propelled worry and then I cannot steal peeks at or dwell on myself any longer, because I reach the spot on Route 22 where I always exhaled those decades of Friday-night drives. It is a place where the stands of big trees on both sides suddenly end and the road opens up into light and sky and farm fields as far as you can see in every direction. This was always my threshold, all those years, the place I'd genuflect; as soon as I saw that opening and the rolling fields beyond, I knew I was almost home. This day, the foreground of the landscape to my east is bare where the alfalfa has been erased, the only trace the marks in the soil where the furrows were. Until your eye reaches the far-off corn, gone pale but still standing, there is next to nothing, mere texture that is barely two-dimensional. But then the ascent begins, and fast: the vertical wall the first far-off row of corn seems to form, and the hard surface its aggregate of countless tops across many rows read as—an earth-toned, mono-chromatic early Cubist work like a 1910 Picasso, but bathed in much older light, the light of the Dutch Renaissance.

THE DAY HAD BEGUN WITH A FLOCK of yellow-shafted northern flickers—*Colaptes auratus*, a common and beautiful woodpecker, though one I have never seen before in more than onesies and twosies, whose light brown back is marked with crescents of black, its paler breast in dramatic black spots. Their species is one of very few woodpeckers on this continent who are strongly migratory. These particular flickers were just stopping in for the local supply of ants in the upper field before continuing their jour-ney, but the resident pileated woodpeckers (*Dryocopus pileatus*)— the largest species by far and very territorial—hadn't seen the interlopers' travel itinerary. And so down the prehistoric-looking pileateds came from the largest trees where they carve giant cavi-ties, drumming incessantly in the most beautiful way to say *go away, this tree's mine*, seeking ants, too, but from the wood, not the soil. Down they came, swooping in with that woodpecker style of flight—its pattern a draped bunting if the movements were each one in a series of connected dots, *swoop, swoop, swoop*—to see what these other feathered ant-eaters were doing below. And then a midair dance of the woodpeckers, accompanied by so many squawking voices. Much commotion, and much comedy— all over some anthills I'm more than happy to share.

To most people fall is a time of departures, of loss, but it is also one of great arrivals: the flickers and migrating warblers and others, albeit only for short visits; the coming of the show of foliar color, when the chlorophyll that is the stuff of active growth fueled by photosynthesis gives way to those extravagantly colored anthocyanins again.

There is a bumper crop of acorns this year—symbols of patience before payoff, yes, since mighty *Quercus* take time, but also perhaps a good omen against a proliferation of lightning if one takes Scandinavian mythology to heart. Oaks were sacred to Thor, the god of lightning and thunder, and medieval citizens brought branches (especially from oaks that had been struck) and later acorns into the house for protection. I am inclined to find solace and good news in all such esoteric trivia, and am stocking up appropriately, filling a bowl and a saucer and a cup on the sideboard full of the preposterously designed creations with their pointed tips, as perfect as if machined, and those beretlike cupules worn jauntily up top.

The compost heap grows full again this next month in an equal and opposite reaction to the folding hand of the played-out garden, reaching its peak of biomass—all those spent vegetables and ornamental foliage and flowers, the raked-up leaves. I do not mourn for what is passing but welcome it, especially this year because somehow in the magical way I think about everything, I think that then and only then, with the full arrival of fall, can I get back in step with a calendar again. This is my time of life—at fifty-five, I am in mid- or even late autumn—and if I am ever going to sync up it will be now. This should be a beat that I can get in step with, then ride along on, and I am listening for cues so I can break back into the conga line—or is it the limbo we are up to here?

There is an extra richness to every fall on this road so far, particularly sweet after our eerily silent spring: Herb and Flora are back, just in from their camp in Maine, where they spend the summers. We quickly caught up with the best stories of the months apart—Herb liked the one of the scat latrine and the coyote urine best, of course, and he liked the bag of sweet potatoes I shared, too, a reversal, since it has always been Herb who has had the luck with them, but not this year. Now we are all back in our spots, ready for whatever's ahead. Soon the mowing decks will come off in favor of the plow blades, and we will dance again.

It may signal a winding down, a senescence of the botanical and animal year, but there is also a madness to the autumn—pink dawns and pinker sunsets and mercurial cold-hot-cold chaos; the first fires; so many small birds swirling around the house on the quickening winds, faster than I can identify them. *Where are you headed, birds? Where?*

The sky is angry, not quite over last night's spat that led to the first good rain in weeks. The man who visited for garden tours in August—the old friend then lost track of and now resurfaced, the one whose hug felt good but who hasn't yet offered another—is visiting again, as he has done most weekends since for a walk or a chat or supper, a gentle messenger sent to teach me how to socialize again, or so I am guessing based on evidence provided so far.

We have just returned from down this beautiful road apiece when we stop to look at the frog ponds out back, drawn to their edges by the sound of the running little waterfalls, and there he is: A male bull, perhaps one of the escapees of May, has moved back in on the overnight storm, apparently in hopes of passing the winter in my apparently just-right muck.

In a rainstorm he departed, and in a rainstorm he returned—after a four-and-one-half month absence, with not so much as a single word of explanation; just that same stupid smile frozen on his face. But I am hearing the Hafiz poem that's been taped to my refrigerator for years:

> *There are different wells within your heart.*
> *Some fill with each good rain,*
> *Others are far too deep for that . . .*

—*THE GIFT*; DANIEL LADINSKY, TRANSLATOR

At first, the young female bull whom the frogboys had deserted, now grown to adult size, wasn't having any, either, and turned her back to him across the pond. Hell hath no fury . . . but only temporarily. We, a man and a woman, watch this amphibian man-and-woman moment together, and then go inside to make supper.

By the next day I see that the two are checking each other out, tucked in beside a flowerpot together, and by next spring—well, you know what will be happening by next spring. Actually, they'll soon be sleeping together in the sludgy stuff at the bottom of the pool for the winter, I predict, though I have it on good authority she's warned him that there will be no monkey business (frogboy business?) until May or June.

She's worth waiting for; I just hope he knows it, and sticks around this time.

This handsome, big male, his chest still slightly tinged with the yellow of mating season and also distinctively freckled, has not been back two days before the word gets out: Good Eats

Over at Margaret's. Just before the dusk takes hold, when the dipping sun is glinting off the windows, the great blue heron lands halfway between me and Buddha, just feet from where the reunited bulls are bobbing aimlessly in the pool. I stand up quickly from the table, indignant, and apparently it is enough; my reflection on the glass startles him, and off he flies as fast as he blew in.

Oh, no, you don't (as if I have any real control of anything, ever—but the preposterousness of the task never stopped this girl from trying). From the barn I drag a load of thick, ten-foot bamboo poles to make an impromptu grating across the pool that hopefully from the sky will read as *this is not water; go away.* I place bars on the watery window into frogland. I do not see the bulls again for two days, apparently until they feel, at last, that the coast is clear. Although they are silent, as they are from September until May or thereabouts, I am glad of their company. They are good listeners—or at least I keep on talking.

That evening, for the second time this week and actually in the eight years we have been together, Jack jumps into my lap and goes promptly and soundly to sleep. He is pondering the coming winter, too; sizing up the best spots, apparently having forgotten about that heated bed in his own cabin. *Do you want to spend the night?* I ask him, and (as ever) *Do you love me?*

As I sit down to breakfast barely twelve hours later, the largest red fox I have ever seen, easily more than twenty pounds, trots across the same route as the heron had, as if on a mission. With colder days showing themselves, I suspect this solitary hunter, too, is digging in here with me—finding that some corner of our shared northeast territory would make the ideal earthen den. Welcome.

*   *   *

"LIBERTY, WHEN IT BEGINS TO TAKE ROOT, is a plant of rapid growth." So said George Washington, though the subject wasn't garlic. It might have been, since garlic cloves set beneath the soil surface in October will show green shoots before winter's hardest freezes buffet us. It is intrepid, even in my harsh-winter zone, sending its tender vanguard to brave whatever comes, a spectacular if slender show of promise.

But then it makes you wait, and not until the next July will you taste it—and then you wait again, as years can pass in the building up of your own stock. A landmark, now: I am celebrating my first fall of garlic independence, like any liberty one achieved through a combination of toil, patience, and a vigilant eye. Growing garlic is dating with an eye to marriage. It can take many years to find the variety that suits you, from among hundreds in cultivation and commerce, and then at least as long again to get in step with each other and work out the particulars of till death us do part.

I have been at it in earnest for four years since I first met German Extra Hardy after wasting much time on less compatible souls like New York White. For a while I thought I had fallen for Russian Red, an almost-as-tough tough character. But how can I explain where I have ended up except to say that the chemistry was just better between me and my German friend?

German Extra Hardy has very long roots to help anchor itself in the ground during winter's repeated deep freezes and alternating thaws. The giant cloves—usually just four or five (sometimes up to seven) to a head—are perfect for someone who goes heavy on the stuff when she cooks. And so we are a match in garden and kitchen, but at four or even five dollars a head for organic bulbs, you want to spend the time bulking up your own supply—not eating it all, and actually not eating any of the best cloves for several years, but saving those fattest, most promising ones to replant as "seed" come October. Eventually, if you choose carefully and cultivate and then cure the crop with diligence, you never order garlic again.

I am there, or will be with the coming harvest of another summer. From the yield of forty-five heads this year, seventy-five of my best cloves are buried several inches in the ground—six inches apart in the row, and rows a foot from each other—and there was plenty for flavoring both the freezers full of soups and sauces and stews so far, with a few dozen cloves (the relative runts) and another dozen full heads to spare. The only vegetable or herb left to plant this season will go in sometime before Thanksgiving, and it will be next spring's spinach. Like the garlic it will be fine beneath the blanket of snow, quietly and secretly holed up away from view but making use of any growing time it can eke out of forgiving moments the coming "dormant" season brings to gain a head start on every other vegetable.

What I like best about plants is that they contain not just the germplasm that will become a future harvest but also the nut of a clever lesson; this is why I tend to anthropomorphize them and regard them among my closest mentors. From garlic comes the discipline of selection—learning how to choose to emphasize the best traits, like an inclination to root well in, while downplaying the less desirable—good guidance for whatever creature we find ourselves incarnated as this time around.

*   *   *

THE SKY IS FALLING! OH, THE WORDS OF WEATHER, how they echo our mental plights: A "complex system" of "upper-level disturbances" converges on us, and with its own violent, two-day-long theatrics takes most of the visual drama away from what was left of fall. It is thirty-five degrees warmer than a week ago, but not for long. I know this game.

Though the twisting road downhill to the tiny post office was thickly slathered with a slick yellow mosaic this morning, each maple leaf among millions playing its part brilliantly, it will not last. The earthen monotone is gaining on us, solidifying its position of incoming ruler of the landscape—and our moods, if it can turn us to the dark side; know that it will try—for many months ahead. All will be laid bare.

The violent storm, the second of the new season, took the maples, the primary fuel of fall's fire here, and then the oaks started to open their fists, too, though much more hesitantly, their attachment to free fall far more tentative. *Open your hands if you want to be held*, the Buddha says, and apparently the oaks can hear him, too. Gradually they learn to let it go, or most of them do, and relax into loss and quieter days, into oneness and communion with all the world's leaves, though whenever the wind picks up the sky fills with flocks of what look like cinnamon-brown birds—the oak leaves, swirling up high on the breeze; perfect papery aircraft with their crispy texture and longer-than-wide profile just made for flight.

A third bull—another male—came in on the latest bruising rain, bringing the total to three adults, and another suitor to fight for my one dear girl when they get their brighter pigments back and raise their voices again in spring. A group of frogs is technically called an army, and mine had deserted me. Now they are gathering again at the front for some tactical maneuver—*are you here in defense of my freedom, big boys?* I suspect it is an under-cover operation, based on the olive-brown dullness of their skin and the increasingly lethargic attitude being demonstrated hereabouts.

Though the storm has passed, there is a sound of rain in the upstairs bathroom; or is it a leak in the aftermath, perhaps? *Always something.* I am only partway up the stairs toward the room before I remember how this latest trickery works: It is October, the sun is shining on one of those Indian summer days that follow such cleansing weather as yesterday's, and that drip-ping sound is so many Asian lady beetles—not drops of water at all, but masses of lady beetles gathering inside the screens, in the window casings, trying to get in past the glass. In their frenzy to find a winter home with me—*there is a crack in everything*, but where?—they crawl up the wooden trim and the mesh screen-ing but at some point on the journey lose their footing and drop onto the sill. And another, and another, and another.

It is raining lady beetles just outside my window.

Masters of adaptation—opportunists, even—it did not take long for the Asian lady beetle (*Harmonia axyridis*) to make its way in America after being imported by the Department of Agricul-ture to control unwanted agricultural pests down South. After mere decades, not millennia, today it calls all parts of the coun-try home, eating aphids and various other small, soft-bodied pests, yes, but also wanting in, where it will dive-bomb its unin-tentional host all winter; foul the bedside glass of water or other food that it drops into with its nasty-tasting secretions; stain whatever it touches. *Ladybug, ladybug, fly away home.* Enough already.

As I type this, one crawls up the left-hand edge of the laptop, and now across the screen. Yes, my unwanted visitor, I know how far you came to get here, and also how much metamorphosing is involved in your impressive life: four distinct phases, from egg to larvae—which molt not once but an astonishing four times to make room for more and more of your growing self—and onward to pupa and then beetle. *So noted; impressive.* Now please, *go fly away home.*

When I climb into bed hours later it is too warm to sleep with much in the way of bedclothes over me, and I am restless. By the predawn it is cold again—or maybe I am just restless and simply choosing to blame the temperature drop, thank you. I awaken with a disturbing urgency; the awareness that I simply must deal with *it*, and fast, before *it* slips away. The snake, that is—the giant snake who is living in a tiny outbuilding in my front yard, an anaconda-size reptile of such girth and length that I am stumped by the task of calculating how many coils it would have to stack itself into to even get inside the shed. The shed that I don't have out front, in the otherwise accurate imagined view just beyond my bedroom windows, with the snake that is neither native nor hardy here spilling out of it, making a deceptively languid game of semiexit and then retreat, a hide-and-go-seek tease as if just playing at showing the fact of all its glory until someone—me—takes proper notice.

My biggest snake dream ever in a lifetime of snake dreams is a whopper, but the gist of the scene that unfolds while I sleep and lingers afterward is about courage, and ethics: Can I live with such a snake, or shall I call for help—and if I do the latter, can I live with the repercussions?

Really, though: Who can I cry out to for rescue this time? Even in my dream, Herb exists in consciousness as my neighbor, a protector, but if I call the dreamworld Herb, I know that he will want to shoot it; snakes that large that close to the house break his safety code, his rules of rural life. If I call the neighbors trained in reptilian relocation, I fear the size of this animal will exceed the capacity of their gear (the same gear they used when we tried to find my real visitor, *Crotalus horridus*, the year before I conjured this newest creature, this supersize serpent).

It is only a matter of weeks or maybe days now before Orion, the hunter, takes his position in the southern night sky right behind the house, a sword by his belt, a club in one hand, a pelt he has taken in the other. He could help me, and knows a thing or two about such tricky situations underfoot. The myth goes that Orion's life ended badly when he stepped on Scorpius, the scorpion, so in sympathy the gods put him and his dogs (Canis Major and Canis Minor) together in the sky, with Taurus the bull and other animals they hunted right nearby; easy pickings. Scorpius, however, was placed all the way across the heavens, keeping Orion out of harm's way forevermore. Who could manage to engineer such guaranteed-safe placements for me, I wonder; can we ever really be safe from all harm, perceived and actual included? *The condition upon which God hath given liberty to man is eternal vigilance.*

Do I kill off this persistent snake of mine, or risk living with it—and just keep watching? I think it stays, a reminder to continue the hunt for wisdom, healing, alchemy. I will keep my frogs, too, another symbol of metamorphosis, and like the snake, of coming into one's creative power. Even my foxes can stay, if I am so blessed with their continued presence, shit and all, those shape-shifters of the hours between night and day who seem to deal in magic. I must stay at peace here with the snakes and with spiders (weavers of illusion, teachers of balance), and the soaring spirits of the birds. I cannot fight, or fear.

From on high it is raining bead-size shit again, but juicy, royal purple shit this time, the lightly used remains of the heavy fruit crop from my many dozens of *Aralia spinosa*, the so-called devil's walking stick, the spiniest and most imposing of botanical creatures and one of my favorite plants of all (but please, do not tell the others). I have a giant glade of it, begun twenty-two years ago from three plants. The paving around the house is stained in purple polka dots, waiting for another good storm to wash it away until this time next year, when the cycle turns past "start" again. Rinse and repeat. And again.

Two male bluebirds and a swirl of warblers arrive with the killing frost this morning, the warblers disinclined to sit still long enough to be keyed out properly. Even in anonymity, they charm me. But it is not mutual, despite a good crop of aralias and holly and crab apples and more to my credit. The lure of somewhere to the south is calling, and they will not stay. The bluebirds, perhaps; for me, there remains no doubt, rooted in as I now am. I am here for the duration. *This is my time of life.*

MY FAVORITE MUG, A GIFT FROM MY OLD-SOUL NIECE several years ago—a big, red-glazed cup with a bright green peace symbol on its side—is cracking, and must be relegated to the reserves, to pencil-cup duty, before the start of a problem proves fatal, shifting from mere hairline to treacherous fault. I need a cup; I cannot sit here and drink tea without a favorite cup, particularly as the days grow colder, and drinking tea is the one consistent bookend of my still somewhat unshapely days.

"We just got those," said the proprietress of the shop called Seed, one of maybe three stores within three quarters of an hour drive that sells dishware at all, let alone something special, something just right. (*Of course you did*, I thought, smiling in tight-lipped silence, *and just for me. In fact, I think you probably named this store just for me. I live in the woods, you know, and grow things.*)

Do you believe in magic? This mug does. (This mug *is*.)

The bewitching vessel is tall and well-proportioned, ample for accommodating the extra-milk way I take my tea. But silhouette wasn't the primary attraction: It was the stylized blue deer romping on each side, their antlers holding fantastical birds or gleaming jewels atop each point, their racks turned into outlandish chandeliers embellished with pulsing, otherworldly ornaments. From the woodland scene that surrounds the deer, polka-dotted, blue-capped magic mushrooms grow from a velvety carpet of moss, and out of hollows in the trunks of the fanciful trees in this crazy, happy forest pokes a face of some exotic bird or another. Even the birds smile.

This electric wilderness is my kind of place. I'll drink to—er, out of—that.

I have been staring outward at my own magic kingdom for twenty months now—yes, blogging and otherwise playing with digital tools, but mostly just looking at the intentional act I have committed in making the garden, juxtaposed as it is against the vast views of nature above and beyond the closer-in contrivance I imposed with shovel and shears. The bigger Garden someone else made—the one of Bible songs I like best when Johnny Cash sings them for me, old-style. *I come to the garden alone*, indeed.

The bigger Garden, capital G, perpetually tries to take over the relatively puny one that I have placed in its shadow. It musters forces far greater than a barn full of tools and these two hands, even with Susan helping part-time—even with a minion, if we had one—will be able to keep at a distance forever. We are small; we are nobody—but when we are out there toiling—turning the compost, harvesting the year's sweet potatoes, planting only the biggest cloves of the previous garlic crop to continue to improve our own strain—we are also part of something infinite.

Our motto here on Maggie's Farm: *In Green We Trust.* I've left my future largely in the hands of *veriditas*—nature's divine healing power, or "green truth" (as the word coined by the twelfth-century mystic-composer-naturalist-philosopher Hildegard von Bingen translates; her music has been mesmerizing me for many years). Plants created the Earth's atmosphere, and therefore invited life as we know it. Even this nonbeliever can believe in that.

But twenty-three years of planting and relentless care, and it could all be gone in a moment—*me, too; me, too*—if I turned my back or closed my checkbook. It would be erased by choking vines of bittersweet and sour grapes, and the rest of the imminent invaders who just watched (laughing their unheard plant laughs) at the way I spent so many days, exerting control in the name of horticulture when all else in life felt so out of control. The property is changed, at least for now, with my living pictures, each fashioned from favorite herbaceous and woody companions, many of them old friends by now, or divisions of old friends who got too weak at the core to soldier on but left behind a division as their legacy—DNA handed down across the generations. Will I do that much in the emotional landscape of those who love me, or (especially childless as I am) will my erasure be as fast and thorough as my garden's once the forces have their way? Bittersweet, indeed.

Inside, the heat is on, clacking and singing each time the antifreeze-filled baseboard fins warm up, a ludicrous sounding but otherwise welcome companion. When I was a weekend guest, the sound seemed irritating, and awakened me repeatedly in the night; now it is just part of the backdrop, the tongue the house speaks to me with in winter, the way the big old locusts outside make snapping noises on the coldest days: startling if you do not know the ropes. Now I do, because now I live here.

The little house is brimming with warm, familiar pictures, too, botanical vignettes of things old and new—some formerly or even partially living, like the dried gourds stacked in the various green majolica footed compotes on the sideboard just across the room to the left from where I work. Each buff-colored skin has grown its own complicated pattern of mold, in grays and black and brown to rusty tones, eccentric but surprisingly organized formations the way frost in its own systematics advances on windowpanes on the harshest days, or crystals aggregate in saturated solutions in the lab.

A twenty-four-pound buckskin-colored Cinderella-type pumpkin has squatter's rights to the living room, her flattened, wheel-shaped body divided into twelve bulging segments. Technically she is still alive, as the seeds inside those hermetic gourds might be, too, even after several years of life indoors. No wonder I am so attracted to them; brittle and dry and not looking as they once did, but inside still alive with promise; my kind of creatures, especially now, when skin-shedding and getting at any remaining viable seeds are all the focus. Cinderella (speaking of the stuff of myths) has been in here eleven months now, I realize, and I suppose I ought to make use of her before she slips into a puddle of her own making, a nasty end to a beautiful creature such as she. We are all perishable, but if I am not alert this plump princess will take the rug and table beneath her with her when she goes. Despite that inclination of theirs, to suddenly go all soft on you, I never met a pumpkin I didn't like.

A haphazard collection of antique children's blocks from mismatched partial sets is stacked in a word salad around the rooms, a 3-D crossword broken free from the grid. Within my daily view: BABE FIRE SOIL. GUT. SHIT. And worse. "Your naughty blocks," a recent guest called them, pointing the way that another child, perhaps jealous at your good toy, might rat you out to Mommy for not sharing. Free speech is welcome inside these walls. O AND CARPE DIEM. MAD.

Christmas ornaments do not come out at Christmas here, necessarily, nor ever all go away. *Hark the herald angel, baby*—which is about the only messenger who has failed to surface since I landed in my new life, come to think of it. Now that would catch my attention, though somehow I cannot picture the herald angel as a drama queen, setting up a scat latrine or ripping anybody's head off—not in that flowing white robe, while holding a long brass horn. Giant mercury-glass kugels bob from the window tops on wrought-iron brackets meant to hold hanging plants; a swag of glittery garland encircles the pie safe in the corner for good measure. Nonstop Noel.

So many colorful plates—the kind you eat from—hang on the walls, and so do hand-colored plates from the very end of the eighteenth century, when destined-to-fail-big-but-beautifully Dr. Robert John Thornton first published the prints from his grand *Temple of Flora*, a homage he produced, incorporating prints by many artists, to the work of Swedish botanist Linnaeus, the father of taxonomy. Nobody noticed them at a nearby winter auction a few years back, and they came home to live with me. The dedication page hangs, framed, over my right shoulder, a message to Thornton's queen, Charlotte, something about conjugal fidelity and patroness of botany, in an exaggeratedly cursive hand.

So what to make of it all, inside and out, what to make of the elements of my exterior and interior viewsheds, especially the souvenirs I still keep tucked farther inside self, the ones we haven't got to yet, that might need a good dusting off? Goodness knows that I have been staring long enough to be entitled to a theory of my own, no? If I am to fashion my own myth—and I believe I must, to go on bravely—is it a modern-day version of Pandora's box that I have opened by leaving management, Manhattan, Martha? A three-foot-tall clay jar balanced in an iron stand is positioned right behind me; poor Pandora (made from clay herself) actually held such a large jar and not a box at all, before she disregarded Zeus's warning and pried the lid off, leaving only hope inside as mankind's solace when all of those evils of the world flew out to haunt us evermore.

Pan = all and *dora* = gifts: It can be tricky to live bestowed with insatiable curiosity, an asset and liability rolled into one tough *bracciole*. Though hers is not my story, I share that trait, at least. It was all my years of "what if?" thinking that got me here, pried by my own ceaseless questioning right out of the self-made and more-familiar groove with all its schedules and infrastructure that both comfort and strangle. I took the lid off, too.

But even so, this is not Pandora's jar, or box.

Or perhaps I have a touch of Circe, if I am to choose among the Greeks, for it was she who lived in a clearing in a tangled, dense woodland; who knew the herbal powers of plants, and was inclined to change men into animals when they misbehaved or otherwise displeased her. (This last bit I am still perfecting, though they sometimes do a pretty good job at it themselves.) Poor Picus, who loved another, became a feathered creature in Ovid's *Metamorphoses*; in *The Odyssey* of Homer, Circe conjured pigs from those who didn't meet with her approval. If the pigskin fits . . . *oink.*

Lately, though, I have come to feel it's more of a *Wunderkammer*, or Cabinet of Curiosities, a clever vessel created by those who were straddling the worlds of older magic and unfolding science in the sixteenth and seventeenth centuries, the ages of discovery and exploration; an often room-size organizing vessel that became the precursor to the museum. The explorers who went out in service to their princes prepared themselves with nets of varying sizes, with boxes and jars and bottles, and with salt and alcohol for the act of preserving treasures like monkey's teeth and dried fishes and fruits, and the skins of alligators.

As I write this, I hear Meryl Streep invoke Karen Blixen: "I have been a mental traveler." Though all I did was show up for each of my days so far, never attempting crude taxidermy during perilous ocean voyages exactly, the device of a *Wunderkammer* will suit me just fine in the continuing transition, I think. *I want people to look and learn*, Peter the Great said around 1714, referring to the *Kunstkammer*, as he knew this cabinet-as-organizing-principle. Sounds good to me, Peter; sounds like a plan: Look and learn.

In my mind's eye I can build a cupboard big enough to hold

all that I am feeling, all that I have collected along the trail so far, and help me gather my thoughts about my very own New World. To hell with psychiatry and life coaching, matchmakers and all of it; this latest conceit will work just fine. Perhaps I have been a bit at sea lately, come to think of it—and hadn't my spam fortune said to cast off the bowline? I should have just read the four-hundred-year-old wisdom of Francis Bacon when I quit my job, instead of taking "The Passion Test" (blushing hotly now at the thought). In 1594 he said that a learned man needs several things: a library, a laboratory, and a garden, and also

> ...a goodly, huge cabinet, wherein whatsoever the hand of man by exquisite art or engine has made rare in stuff, form or motion; whatsoever singularity, chance and the shuffle of things has produced; whatsoever Nature has wrought in things that want life and may be kept; shall be sorted and included.

"Chance and the shuffle of things," indeed. Such a splendid compartment, if only in imagination, I, too, can employ it to come to grips with the disparate treasures of my journey to date, placing each one in its proper spot inside, then moving the pieces around until the story they tell looks like one I can live with.

I will be a mental cabinetmaker.

How many sections shall there be, and what goes where? I love a taxonomic puzzle; the Order Beds at Kew or Cambridge or Oxford in England were always my favorite gardens, places where the genetic relationships between plants—their pollen granules and other matters best left to electron microscopes—determined their placement, not a mere matter like aesthetics, with all its bent toward subjectivity and even raw emotion. What blend of system and fantasy can I make of a collection now grown to seven weasel tails; a pile of egg-shaped white gourds so well named as the heirloom variety Nest Egg; various cast-off snakeskins (*ack!* I should have saved the fallen hairs from that country cut); maybe mouthy, incessant, insistent Jack himself? There are marbled, purple and black runner beans, offered up spontaneously when their rough tan pods finally allowed it and split; hawk feathers found in the driveway; dozens of vaguely heart-shaped stones—gifts from others, or from the overland trail of my own life's travels.

There is the oval cardboard frame, just six and a half by five inches, painted dark green then mottled with a spritz of gold spray paint for good measure, that surrounds one of my early masterpieces. It holds a crayon drawing of myself—arms raised up as if in a hurrah—standing beside a little green house with bright red trim. The sky, all yellow, predicts a positive outcome. I could not have been more than six when I created it, and for forty-eight more years I waited to stand in the sun beside just such a Christmas-colored house where every day is an increasing gift of awareness of the present. Yes, the drawing is definitely part of the cabinet's contents, and the story; it shall have a shelf of its own, for just in this very instant I realize that it is where the trip to here began.

Epilogue

It cannot be done all at once. To overcome vertigo—
the power of the abyss—one must tame it, cautiously.

—PHILIPPE PETIT, *TO REACH THE CLOUDS*

IN 1942, A HARVARD MEDICAL PROFESSOR entered into scientific literature the conviction that one can, in fact, die from fright—from what Walter Bradford Cannon, MD, labeled "Voodoo Death." I know I almost did: almost shriveled up and perished from being afraid to jump ships from a luxury liner into a lopsided-but-nevertheless-floating rowboat. I am fascinated that Cannon was the same man who twenty-five or so years earlier had described and coined the fight-or-flight mechanism, another tug-of-war that was also surely at work in me, sympathetic neurons ever a-popping. But there I go thinking again.

My nonstop string of days here in the little house began with writing a fear list—a long one, remember?—and so far, so good: None of the objects of my terror has come back to bite me, or at least not in any way that proved fatal or left otherwise permanent marks. I still have all my parts, but fear's a scary thing.

Even now, two years into working on my reactions to lightning and venomous serpents, I still stare at birds between sentences, just as when I started typing. There have been some incremental if not impressive improvements logged, but it was my overactive thinking mind that I should have had on the top of that fear list, I now believe. I work nonstop, as I will for the rest of my days, trying to balance my inclination toward retreating into the comfort of thinking mind against my somewhat-heightened awareness that such a place is nowhere near "good enough" to inhabit (thank you, Dr. Goudard; that rating system is now my DNA). But just go sit somewhere and try to do that—the very word *try* an impediment to flow—just try to stop thinking all the time. See how tricky this is (she says, laughing at the hard facts of humanness)? Even when you pick the best seat in the house, as I did, and one with absorbing, meditative views, settling into solitude is no express train to serenity.

From my seat I have become intensely aware of just how thoroughly we live in a world that fosters left-brain development—logic, rationality, and analysis, specifically. It is a wonder that its counterpart just across the corpus callosum—the right brain and especially the right temporal lobe—has not become a vestigial organ, I sometimes think. *Oops*, there's the *T* word again. Any sense of connection comes from the intuitive, more holistically oriented right side, and connection (odd as it may sound) has been the one true mission of my unplugging and apparent disconnection from the old.

I suppose the span of days has been spent in a kind of divination—looking for knowledge of the future without "real" things like a business plan or school curriculum or any of the maps that life's powerful grid, and I, provided for me prior. More all the time I feel at home with letting the hours and even a whole day unfold, taking reassurances where and when I can get them, from whomever surfaces as the latest in the series of messengers. I recently felt, for instance, as if I had been saved by the bell (or was it a gong?) when the cover of *Tricycle: The Buddhist Review* seemed to say that I am on the right track with its encouraging 2009–2010 winter issue headline: *Doing nothing can make you wise.*

Hoping so over here; really hoping so. But doing nothing except trying to be still can also make you sedentary, or at least it can in winter, and so I am now shacked up not just with Jack the Demon Cat but with a cute, cheap, easy little pedometer I have invited into my life. Like my increasingly gray hair, it serves as warning to get a move on.

Let's say, then, that the trip so far has been one part my style of divination and one part the suspension of disbelief. Many days I cannot believe how much stock I put in randomnesses that befall me—what comes out of the radio, who lopes or flies into the yard—magical thinking of one kind or another. For better or worse, this is how I live now, no longer waiting to be reassured by the percentage of my annual bonus or any other tangible marker of progress like a job promotion. Randomness, along with instinct and, if you are lucky, scrappiness, are what you have left when you take the detour that I did. I take comfort in the knowledge that the cultivation of chance worked so well for much more gifted individuals such as the late composer John Cage or for George Harrison, lovers of the I Ching and delighters in come what may—and hey, the soundtracks of their life adventures sound just fine to me. My worn 1981 Bollingen Series edition of the ancient text, with a set of old coins tucked into a tiny homemade pocket taped inside the back cover, sits out in the living room with all the rest of the printed wisdom I marked up with pencil scrawls while I was treading water, worrying about my ability to really swim alone.

"I think everything in the world is interesting," said Cage, "and I think our minds tend to narrow the possibilities and to think this one is better than that one. And when we use chance operations we give up the idea of limiting things to the best; we take everything." Let it rip, brother.

A lot still happens in a quieter life—particularly if you stand up occasionally and make your way to the post office. A package arrived the other day from the brother of my friend Erica. David is a painter, and though we have never met, he's some form of family as a consequence of my relationship to her—more now than ever. The box contained an oil on canvas, a panoramic image twice as wide as it is tall, the way sights are framed when you're looking out the windshield of your car, for instance, like I used to at the very spot the painting depicts. The subject is the threshold spot, the place on Route 22 where I used to finally start to breathe all those hurry-hurry-gotta-get-there Friday nights, the place where the woods open up into an expanse of sensuous, rolling fields. David, who lives nearly a thousand miles away, has perfectly captured my favorite spot, godlight and all.

It seems that Erica had sent him an iPhone image of it, though even she did not know of its role in this book (see page 223, the first rural haircut scene). If my little framed crayon drawing of the red and green house was the beginning, the mental image of the spot was my beacon all those schizophrenic years, too. Now I have it, like a Russian icon painting (minus the Russian part). The *Wunderkammer* is filling up.

I HEARD NOT LONG AGO FROM JONATHAN that he would be in town again, and cashed in the final credit on account at my old spa refuge—money left on deposit after a previous stay was cut short, my symbolic last lifeline in this one-woman reality / game show. Off I went, actually leaving the house for a destination beyond "downtown" Copake Falls for the first time since I cannot recall when. *What shall I wear?*

As soon as I arrived at the resort, where I had hoped a few more lightbulbs might go on in my head during precious conversation with my visiting friend, the lights went out. *No, really.* The facility experienced its first extended power outage since— guess when?—the date of my previous stay a year before, when that big, pounding storm had darkened it for hours. Woo-woo; another exploration of powerlessness—or is it a reminder of my own enormous power? (Kidding; even my extended solitude hasn't cost me all perspective on my place in the larger universe, though thinking that way occasionally reminds us of the importance of belief in self, and of volition.) Whatever the cause, it seemed as if things were right on track, and starting where we left off. But as that drama subsided, what came clear was this: If I have often played the misfit, this was my starring role.

I was wildly restless, and missed Jack—who had been allowed overnight stays in the Big House a few times before my departure, his first; we both bowed to a nasty bout of high winds and single digits. I wonder if he felt as uncomfortable on those sleepovers as I do here in this fancy big rented bed. Was he thinking of the heated pad back in the doghouse-like covered box inside his cabin across the yard? Oops, there I go, being more shamanic than sensible and scientific, once more imposing my anthropomorphic slant. Or maybe that's a good thing, but the teacher of the bird-behavior course I am taking online with the Cornell Laboratory of Ornithology would not think so. (Yes, I am taking a class— and also reading up to prepare to grow my first mushrooms, and taking ever longer walks—things I *never had time* for.)

"Thinking of animals like people is misleading and unhelpful, and offers no assistance in understanding animal behavior," says Kevin McGowan, a noted ornithologist and leading expert on crows, typing his admonishment into the online forums that simulate our classroom discussion. "Thinking of people as animals with the same survival goals can provide profound insights into what we do." Fact—but I cannot help myself. This latest teacher would not approve one bit of the talks with Jonathan, but no matter; the mix of elements and educations, however disparate, that I choose to make the curriculum of my life is my choice now, and it hopefully redefines Liberal Arts.

I know McGowan is right, but here's the thing: I am as eager to know definitively why some male and female ducks bob their heads rhythmically (to get in step for mating) as I am to know why three wrens showed up from nowhere and sang from that very same spot on New Year's Day for the second year in a row (pure magic). Who, what, when, where, why—and woo-woo. Those are the questions I have, and more, most of them beginning with "I wonder…"

I do not do all the questioning; these days, people still ask me things like how I dared leave the land of plenty: *What about health insurance? What about security? Weren't you afraid?* (The local Chamber of Commerce saved me. I don't know. Yes, but not as afraid as I was of drying up and blowing away.)

People ask me what I miss in just the way they always have about what cravings live on through the thirty-plus meatless years (bacon, meatloaf, and boatfuls of gravy is the easy answer in the latter case). But what do I miss about that other life? I haven't got an answer there, except that I feel hungry for more delicious, sustaining time with my former neighbor, Marco. That has been the biggest price of my decision.

People ask if I am lonely, and that is the easiest common question of all. (No, quite simply; no. I am happy indulging my many curiosities, and talking mostly to animals. The fact of having other souls here—each with its own breath, voice, hungers—makes all the difference.)

WHEN MARTHA SAID "LEARN SOMETHING NEW EVERY DAY," did she mean things like these?

That I am no flatlander, no matter where I was born.

That you have to be a little brave to make changes, to try something new, but you don't have to be fearless (even Philippe Petit did not claim to be so).

That there is no possibility of achieving a perfect score; you cannot have everything; the sky is not the limit (though spending time looking at it would be well advised). *He who knows where to stop may be exempt from danger*, said Lao Tzu. Yup.

That I will be the grill cook at the annual town barbecue as long as they will have me, as long as we both shall live.

That if you leave one of Jack's discarded bodies on the porch or in the pathway, someone will clean it up for you; the food chain does dishes, if not the windows he scuffs with his paws, beseeching me to let him back inside.

That there is a business opportunity in a truly effective pet-hair remover. I have them all by now, and all fall short.

And this:

That I am a cat person. I learned this just the other day, when

I grabbed Jack off the kitchen floor and was spontaneously over-taken with laughter, clutching him to me. "I can't believe how much I love you," I blurted right out loud, before the thinking mind had a chance to stifle that declaration.

Speaking of love—when I went to visit him the last time, Jonathan wanted to tell me about his mother, who when she was widowed (after decades in service to marriage and family) really rebounded with a new vitality for life. Happy as the sons were for her apparent adjustment and even invigoration, they wondered to each other with concern that she had no "love in her life." Eventually they asked her about it—didn't she want to meet a man again, to fall in love?

"Fall in love?" she replied, slightly incredulous. "No, not really, I don't—because I am in love with my life."

Margaret Roach, March 2010

Acknowledgments

The eleventh-century sage Atisha taught the principle of *be grateful to everyone*, as you have heard me say, but perhaps that blanket expression—a good one to try to live by otherwise—will not suffice in this instance, on these particular pages. It works just fine on the chalkboard in my kitchen, where it has been inscribed for what seems like ever.

I wish to express gratitude to every messenger who has tried to get me to listen; especially the ones whose yes-you-can words I doubted at first. Yes, you told me so. The front-row cheering section of such guidance counselors has long included photographer Erica Berger, the only friend a woman ever needs, and Marco Polo Stufano, my garden mentor and sometime surrogate father-husband-brother. Along with my fierce, red-haired writer sister, Marion, a four-time author who teaches (yup) memoir writing and trotted out just the right tip every time I hit a wall; my astonishing niece, Grace; and my brother-in-law, Rex Smith, the only man who could have weathered twenty-plus years of being related to the Roach girls, Erica and Marco have formed the family of my adult life.

If not for Martha Stewart, I might never have thought in such "why not?" style. Consider this: Martha started *Martha Stewart Living* magazine when she was almost fifty. Though I had to walk away from her world to be here, she is never far from my thoughts, and her example to *learn something new every day* is a mantra (I can spell that word correctly now). What my maternal grandmother, Marion Rollins Zillmann, had first told me was worth learning—plants and collecting and cooking and home economics of all sorts—Martha confirmed, and even paid me to explore. I am better for both of their influences. Busy hands *are* happy hands.

Other guides you have already met: Herb and Flora Bergquist, whose image should be next to the dictionary entry defining *neighbor*; Dr. Eric V. Goudard, MD (not his real name), forever the Big Cheese; Mr. Spirituality Jonathan Ellerby, PhD; rural grooming adviser Bob Hyland (and to his partner Andrew Beckman, for keeping an eye on both of us). The English doodler Andre Jordan is the only other person whose work is allowed on my precious and personal garden blog. Enough said. The madcap vacation times I spent here in the garden with Glenn Withey and Charles Price helped make the view worth staring at. I'd better formally also thank Susan Ziobron, gardening sidekick and taskmaster, but I will not dwell on her too long or she will be wanting a tractor of her own and other benefits the revised budget precludes.

The entire hamlet of Copake Falls, New York—or Cupcake Falls, as I refer to it—has made me feel welcome, and I embrace you. (And by the way, does anybody know where to get a good deal on fully guaranteed lightning rods, or have tips for outfoxing foxes?)

Writer-and-more Kurt Andersen has not stopped coaxing me for more than thirty years; his wife, writer Anne Kreamer, added her voice to the mix shortly thereafter. Both of these veteran dropouts from corporate culture have listened, urged, inspired, and sometimes downright confronted. Thank you both.

My longtime friend and literary agent Kris Dahl (as in "you're too old to bank on only one thing, so let's try a few" Kris, *whoa, Nellie!*) is tough and tender as can be, the right aspect surfacing at the right time. Thanks also to her assistant, Laura Neely.

What I feared most professionally besides financial ruination was working in isolation, without the sounding board of colleagues. That was solved when Kris got me in front of Deb Futter and her team at Grand Central Publishing. How astonishing to find an editor who collected heart-shaped stones (as I do) and has a weekend house not so far down the road; who "gets it" about both the yearning and the fear (and is as fussy as I am about Dustbusting and more that we will keep to ourselves). Watch out, Deb, or you will find yourself on coyote-impersonation duty before too long, now that you have the 101 handbook.

Deb's colleagues at Grand Central have each been just as patient, particular, and delightful to work with. Art director Diane Luger performed cover heroics, and it was a treat to share the garden and a big bowl of homemade soup with someone with her fantastic eye. Editorial assistant Dianne Choie has an uncanny way of keeping things strictly on the tracks but at the same time being someone you are always glad to hear from—how do you do that, Dianne? Executive director of publicity Matthew Ballast charmed me right away with his polite refusal to answer my impatient questions about "the plan" until he had read my book and properly gotten to know me. No formulaic, one-size-fits-all approaches fly in Matthew's way of thinking, as he and senior publicist Erica

Gelbard (a gardener!) would prove in helping bring *And I Shall Have Some Peace There* out of hiding, no longer my little secret at the dining table. The quiet but essential dialogue played out in e-mail and blue-penciled Post-it notes with senior production editor Mari Okuda and copy editor Christine Valentine were more blessings in the happy chain. Magicians, all.

Speaking of a belief in magic, Dhana Lamabore and the other sons and daughters of Birta Deurali, Nepal, many of them people of the Tamang race, have blessed me with the inspiration of their friendship for more than five years. *Namaste! Phyafulla!*

No woman is an island, especially when she has the open-source WordPress community, whose poetic code empowers me to stay vitally connected and communicative even in my relative isolation. Without web designer and fellow corporate dropout Kenneth B. Smith, I would never have had such a joyous immersion into newness. Web developer Brad Williams and his team completed the picture. *Semper fi*, brothers.

You do not walk away from a regular paycheck without counsel about the practicalities, and Donald Schwarz, my lifelong accountant; Bert Halliday, longtime financial adviser; and attorney Adam Ritholz, a fellow Leonard Cohen addict, have combined to parent me in the ways of budgets and spreadsheets and contracts so that I could try flying *sola* even in a year of crashes. *Whee!* They knew the value I placed on finding my voice again, and that it exceeded the bottom line of any balance sheet, even one that didn't exactly add up.

My friends on Twitter, Facebook, and the blogs remind me nonstop that even when I do not open the gate for a week or longer, I am not alone. When I started my book proposal, A Way to Garden dot com had fewer than one thousand comments; a year and a half later, as I do these acknowledgments, we are passing eleven thousand and gaining fast. I suspect by publication date to double that, because we just cannot seem to shut up about plants, plants, plants. My "sisters" in The Sister Project dot com, Anastasia Smith, Paige Smith Orloff, and my real sister, Marion, have been my writers' group and virtual watercooler companions. Thank you, chiquitas.

EACH PERSON IN THIS LAST GROUP knows his or her contribution: Matt Armendariz, Dora Cardinale, Amy Conway, Rich Fontaine, Mark Gerow, Maxwell and Sara Kate Gillingham-Ryan, Kelly Hagan, Adrian Higgins, Jane Kasten, Pam Kueber, Steve and Doone Marshall, Charity Curley Mathews, Alicia Matusheski, Sarah McColl, Tom Prince, Debra Puchalla, Anne Raver, Kevin Ryder, Evelyn Santoro, Laura Schmidt, Susan Schneider, Dan Shaw, Kathy Slobogin, Lauren Stanich, and John Trexler.

And then there are the other inhabitants of "my" actual garden, each in his own way an extraordinary guide. *Attention! Attention!:*

The fox, a forest dweller who knows the woods intimately, a monogamous species but one that prefers to live five months of the year alone. In foxland, men are called dogs and women vixens; the Mayans associate the fox with writing.

The frogs, symbols of metamorphosis and of coming into creative power, mythical controllers of the weather. Like the birds and the rattlesnake, they are twice-borns, starting as eggs.

The birds, masters of the air and breath, apt readers of the weather, who know when to migrate and when to stay put.

The snakes, symbols of rebirth and transformation, who open

up to take in and swallow whole all that is needed to survive and thrive.

The weasels, graceful, silent, and solitary—but also ferocious—creatures that can find their way even in the tightest spots.

The cat, with its spirit of independence, its curiosity, its nine lives; a symbol of the realm of magic.

Good teachers, all.

The Lake Isle of Innisfree
by William Butler Yeats

I will arise and go now, and go to Innisfree,
And a small cabin build there, of clay and wattles made:
Nine bean-rows will I have there, a hive for the honeybee,
And live alone in the bee-loud glade.

And I shall have some peace there, for peace comes dropping slow,
Dropping from the veils of the morning to where the cricket sings;
There midnight's all a glimmer, and noon a purple glow,
And evening full of the linnet's wings.

I will arise and go now, for always night and day
I hear lake water lapping with low sounds by the shore;
While I stand on the roadway, or on the pavements grey,
I hear it in the deep heart's core.